Getting into University

Psychology Courses

Dr Konstantinos Foskolos

16th edition

Getting into University: Psychology Courses

This 16th edition published in 2026 by Trotman, an imprint of Trotman Indigo Publishing Ltd, 18e Charles Street, Bath BA1 1HX.

© Trotman Indigo Publishing Ltd 2026

Author: Dr Konstantinos Foskolos
13th–15th edns: Dr Konstantinos Foskolos
12th edn: Jody-Helena Williams
11th edn: John Cooter
10th edn: John Cooter and Joel Rickard
7th–9th edns: Maya Waterstone
5th–6th edns: James Burnett and Maya Waterstone
1st–4th edns: MPW

British Library Cataloguing in Publication Data
A catalogue record for this book is available from the British Library

Paperback ISBN 978 1 911724 95 7
eISBN 978 1 911724 96 4

All rights reserved. This book is sold subject to the condition that it shall not, by way of trade or otherwise, be lent, resold, hired out or otherwise circulated without the publisher's prior written consent in any form of binding or cover other than that in which it is published and without a similar condition including this condition being imposed on the subsequent purchaser. No part of this publication may be reproduced, stored in a retrieval system or transmitted in any form or by any means, electronic and mechanical, photocopying, recording or otherwise without prior permission of Trotman Indigo Publishing.

Every effort has been made to trace copyright holders and to obtain their permission for the use of copyright material. The publisher apologises for any errors or omissions, and would be grateful to be notified of any corrections that should be incorporated in future editions of this book.

The authorised representative in the EEA is Easy Access System Europe Oü (EAS), Mustamäe tee 50, 10621 Tallinn, Estonia.

Printed and bound in the UK by 4edge Ltd, Hockley, Essex.

 All details in this book were correct at the time of going to press. To keep up to date with all the latest news and updates and to access the online resources that accompany this book, use this QR code or visit **www.trotman.co.uk/pages/getting-into-online-resources**

Contents

About the author	vi
Acknowledgements	vii
About this book	viii
Introduction	**1**
Entry grades needed for a successful application	1
1| What psychology is really about	**3**
Explaining complex behaviours	3
Psychological experiments	7
Scientific methods	9
The rise of neuroscience	9
The study of individual differences	10
Psychotherapy	11
What is psychology really like to study?	12
Why is psychology so popular?	15
2| Careers in psychology	**17**
Professional psychology	18
Psychologists in teaching, lecturing and research	26
Other psychologist roles	27
Roles in psychology not involving a psychology degree	31
Other psychology-related careers	32
Transferable skills	33
3| Work experience	**36**
Choosing the right kind of work experience	36
Making the most of your work experience	37
Work experience and your personal statement	40
When to arrange work experience	41
How to arrange work experience	42
Work experience interviews	46
4| Degree programmes in psychology	**47**
BA or BSc?	48
General or specialised?	48
Single subject, joint or modular?	49
Full time or sandwich?	49
A year abroad?	50
Degree course content	50
Degree courses in Ireland	53
Choosing a university: making a shortlist	55

	How to decide where to apply	56
	Finding out more	59
5|	**The UCAS application**	**60**
	Planning your application	60
	The UCAS application	61
	Completing your UCAS application	63
	Admissions tests	65
	I've applied! What next?	67
	Taking a gap year	68
6|	**The personal statement**	**71**
	How to structure the personal statement	71
	Sample personal statements	75
	Applying for different courses	79
	General tips	79
	Applying for joint honours courses	81
7|	**Succeeding in your interview**	**82**
	Preparation for interviews	82
	General hints for interviews	83
	Specimen interview questions	86
	Asking questions of your own	89
	The interview itself: general reminders	89
8|	**Non-standard applications**	**91**
	Mature students	91
	International students	93
	Students with disabilities and special educational needs	96
9|	**Results day**	**98**
	When the results are available	98
	What to do if you have no offers: UCAS Extra	98
	What to do if things go wrong during the exams	99
	What to do on results day	99
	What to do if you exceeded the grades that you expected	100
	What to do if you have no confirmed offers	101
	UCAS Clearing	101
	If you decide to retake your A levels	102
	If you decide to reapply	103
10|	**Fees and funding**	**104**
	Fees	104
	Living expenses	105
	Funding your studies	106
	Alternative help with fees and funding	108
	Funding for postgraduate courses	109
	Studying overseas	109

11|	**Further information**	**111**
	British Psychological Society (BPS)	111
	Advance HE	112
	Other useful organisations	112
	General university guides	113
	Psychology texts	113
	Useful websites	115
12|	**Glossary**	**116**
	Abbreviations	**118**

About the author

Dr Konstantinos Foskolos is Head of Psychology and Sociology at Mander Portman Woodward's London College. After studying communication and mass media at the National and Kapodistrian University of Athens, he studied for a master's in evidence-based social intervention at the University of Oxford and then two further master's degrees in psychology and child development at University College London. He also completed a doctorate with a specialisation in child psychopathology at the University of Oxford. He is a Chartered Psychologist, a published researcher and accredited member of the British Psychological Society. He is also a qualified teacher and examiner, and has been teaching psychology since 2010.

Acknowledgements

I am grateful for the help provided by Trotman Education and MPW, who allowed me the opportunity to edit this current edition. I am also grateful to those who worked on the earlier editions. Thank you also to the British Psychological Society, whose excellent website and range of publications made the job of writing this guide much easier, to Advance HE, to the academics who contributed quotes and to UCAS. Special thanks to Dr Philippa East for her interview and permission to publish her journey from a psychology undergraduate to a Chartered Psychologist. Finally, I would like to thank former students, academic tutors and admission officers who have provided quotes and sample personal statements for this edition, and to acknowledge the many students I have guided through the UCAS application process over the years. Much of the advice in this book is a product of what I have learned from these experiences and I hope that the reader will benefit.

Dr Konstantinos Foskolos
March 2026

About this book

Deciding what to study after A levels is a daunting task. There are already numerous books, guides and leaflets available to help you make your choice. So why bother to write yet another? *Getting into University: Psychology Courses* is, as the title suggests, specifically for people wanting to do psychology at degree level, and so it tells you exactly what you need to know to get onto the course of your choice.

This book is divided into 12 chapters, which aim to cover three major areas when applying for a degree in psychology.

1. A clear and concise introduction to a subject that students might want to make a career out of.
2. Information on entry requirements, the length and content of the various courses on offer and some indication of what it is like to study psychology.
3. Guidelines on making your UCAS application, getting work experience, writing your personal statement and preparing for an interview.

The 12 chapters discuss the following:

Chapter 1 – What psychology is really about – provides information on what the subject is really about and the different areas of psychology you will study as part of a degree course.

Chapter 2 – Careers in psychology – looks at the different careers a psychology degree might lead to, either as one of several types of professional psychologist, or in many other fields such as marketing, IT, teaching or social work.

Chapter 3 – Work experience – gives advice on work experience: how to choose it, how to arrange it and how to use it in your university application.

Chapter 4 – Degree programmes in psychology – presents an overview of the different types of psychology degree programme on offer and the expected course content.

Chapter 5 – The UCAS application – takes you through the UCAS application process, with particular emphasis on psychology.

Chapter 6 – The personal statement – gives general guidance on drafting a personal statement and specific advice for psychology.

Chapter 7 – Succeeding in your interview – supplies some advice on preparing for and attending interviews, where these are part of a university's selection process.

Chapter 8 – Non-standard applications – is for international students and mature students who may be making a 'non-standard' application.

Chapter 9 – Results day – looks at the options you might have on results day and explains what you will need to do depending on whether you are holding an offer or not and whether you have met the grades of any offer.

Chapter 10 – Fees and funding – explains the current fees and funding arrangements for UK universities.

Chapter 11 – Further information – gives contact details for useful organisations as well as a background reading list for psychology.

Chapter 12 – Glossary – if you are puzzled about any of the words used in the book, look here for an explanation.

This book is intended to complement, not replace, existing publications, many of which are included in the reading list at the end of the guide. If, after you have read the following chapters, your decisions have been eased in any way, its goal will have been achieved.

I hope that after reading the following chapters you will have developed a better understanding of what a psychology degree is all about, a thorough knowledge of the application process and a realistic appreciation of your options on graduating.

Introduction

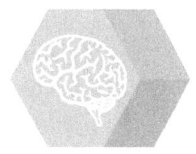

Psychology is a very popular subject at university. According to UCAS data, there were 139,965 undergraduate applications to psychology courses in 2024. Psychology remains one of the most popular degree course options in the UK, along with engineering and technology, computing, business and management and nursing. This is because psychology offers a number of well-defined career paths within its field, as well as being perceived by employers in general as a valuable qualification, as it combines scientific analysis, mathematical skills and the requirement to be able to write coherent and structured essays.

Furthermore, many applicants have very clear ideas about which universities they wish to target. Some of the most popular universities have up to 20 applications for every place, although that needs to be seen in the context that each applicant for psychology can apply to five courses, and so applicants need to think carefully about the strategies they are going to adopt in order to maximise their chances. While there are a great many universities offering psychology, you are by no means guaranteed a place if you apply. This is why this book has been written: to give prospective psychology students advice about making a successful and convincing application.

Entry grades needed for a successful application

As with other degree subjects, the grades required for entry to degree courses in psychology vary from one university to another. Like most degree courses, psychology is very competitive, and many institutions can require top grades at A level. Entry requirements may vary from DDE to A*AA depending on the institution. Typically, the older established universities may ask grades of A*AA to AAA, whereas some of the newer universities may have lower entry requirements based on points. Most universities and colleges require at least BBB for a psychology course. Information and an online points calculator can be found on the UCAS website: www.ucas.com/ucas/tariff-calculator.

Other attributes required could include having an inquisitive attitude, logical and systematic thinking and a genuine enthusiasm for the subject.

> 'Psychology is mind-blowing! It's like uncovering the secrets of why we behave the way we do. It's fascinating exploring the human brain

and figuring out how thoughts, feelings, and behaviours all connect. It is like a puzzle where every piece is a different aspect of our minds, and when you start putting them together, you see this whole picture of how we tick. Plus, it's not just theories – you can actually apply what you learn to real life, understanding people better and even helping them out. It's an evidence-based scientific subject with practical applications to help those in need. And I want to be part of this world!'

Alice

Given the statistical component of most degree courses, admissions tutors will also expect applicants to have a reasonable pass grade in GCSE mathematics. However, you must ensure you check the GCSE mathematical requirement for your choice of universities as the expected grades can vary from a 7/A to a 4/C.

Applicants often need to demonstrate good numeracy and literacy skills, as well as the ability to handle scientific concepts. Biology, Mathematics, English, History, Economics and similar arts and social science subjects are all useful preparation.

British Psychological Society, 2023

A previous qualification in psychology is not normally required for entry to a psychology degree course, but you may find that having GCSE, A level or equivalent in psychology gives you a head start when you begin your degree. There are also universities that require students to have at least one science A level to study psychology. The Russell Group website 'Informed Choices' (www.informedchoices.ac.uk/) suggests that universities may ask for an A level in either biology, chemistry, maths/further maths or physics to study psychology. This is supported by a survey by the Psychology Education Board of the British Psychological Society (BPS, 2023), which confirmed that although students do not necessarily have to complete psychology at A level or Scottish Higher qualification to study it at university, many institutions require at least one science A level subject. Please check the particular requirements of each university course.

TIP!

Work experience is always helpful in supporting an application, as this demonstrates a genuine interest in psychology. Working in a school, nursing home or other care-centred environment will show the admissions tutor that you have really considered your degree choice. Work experience in business organisations can help too, for example in human resources, marketing or customer relations departments. See Chapter 3 for more details.

1 | What psychology is really about

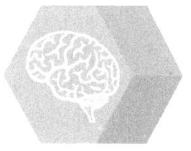

Psychology is the scientific study of brain, mind and behaviour and is an incredibly popular, increasingly competitive course of study at university. Its popularity is fuelled in part by the growing demand for psychology graduates across a wide range of occupations, from health professions, to human resources, to marketing and communications, to IT. Students love studying psychology because it is eye opening, scientifically rigorous and readily applicable to life. Students are given the tools that allow them to see human relations and human behaviour through a special kind of lens, one that aims to give legitimate, evidence-based explanations for behaviour, rather than explanations based on common sense, proverbs or other metaphors. It is said that we are all 'naive psychologists', in that we all have our own explanations for various human behaviours. The trained psychologist, however, typically has three predominant qualities: a natural empathy, a strong background in scientific and statistical methods and a drive to improve his/her own understanding that persists across a lifetime. The aim of this chapter is to give you an insight into some of the typical psychological research you are likely to study in the course of a degree programme.

Explaining complex behaviours

Psychologists endeavour to explain behaviour, and no explanation is ever simple. One way of understanding this is to consider the case of schizophrenia. Schizophrenia is a severe mental disorder characterised by false perceptions of reality, disorganised thought processes and disruption of normal emotions and actions. For example, a normal action for many people is to self-talk while walking or lying in bed as part of their daily planning or reflection; however, schizophrenics perceive these voices as an external voice intruding into their mind. These voices are usually negative, crude and insulting and form running commentaries on the sufferer's behaviour.

According to the World Health Organization (2025), there are more than 23 million people (1 in 345) suffering from schizophrenia. Schizophrenia often begins in late adolescence or early adulthood. Although it affects men and women equally, the age of onset is usually earlier in men than in women. The frequency of symptoms varies in individuals: some patients may experience only one psychotic episode in their whole life; others may have frequent episodes, but are responsive to medication and so live a relatively normal life; while those who experience frequent episodes but are non-responsive to medication remain severely disturbed.

One of the main issues psychologists face in the diagnosis of schizophrenia include comorbidity, symptom overlap, gender bias and cultural bias.

- **Comorbidity:** when patients may have more than one disorder.
- **Symptom overlap:** when symptoms of one disorder appear in the diagnosis of another disorder.
- **Gender bias:** when one gender tends to be pathologised more than the other.
- **Cultural bias:** when one culture tends to be pathologised more than others.

Comorbidity

Comorbidity means that patients may have more than one disorder at the same time as suffering from schizophrenia. For example, Buckley and colleagues (2009) found that 50% of schizophrenics suffered from depression (episodes of low mood), while 47% had a substance abuse diagnosis. Therefore, having simultaneous disorders suggests that schizophrenia may not be a wholly separate disorder.

Symptom overlap

Also, different disorders share common symptoms. For instance, mania (heightened state characterised by great excitement, delusions and over-reactivity), cognitive deficits and hallucinations (distortion of a sensory experience that appears to be real but it is not, as it is created in the mind) are not only symptoms of schizophrenia but also of bipolar depression (depression characterised by episodes of low mood as well as episodes of mania). This may make the diagnosis of schizophrenia less accurate.

Gender bias

In 2003, Heinz Häfner carried out a literature review and found that men and women were at equal risk of developing schizophrenia. However, if clearer diagnostic criteria were applied the number of female sufferers became much lower and the number of male sufferers was more than twice that of females. For example, clinicians fail to consider that males suffer more negative symptoms than women; and have worse recovery rates, higher relapse rates and higher levels of substance abuse. This means that clinicians do not take into account all symptoms and so their diagnosis may not be valid.

Cultural bias

The cultural background of patients should be taken into account before making a diagnosis. Luhrmann and colleagues (2014) showed that schizophrenic patients in California had negative feelings about their voices, whereas in India and Ghana patients had a more constructive relationship with their voices.

What causes atypical behaviour?

A vast amount of research study is focused on the causes of the disorder. We can all present numerous common-sense explanations, such as it is learnt behaviour from family members, influences from the media or perhaps there is a genetic link. While psychological theories consider all these explanations carefully, some explanations lack strong scientific evidence. Psychology is a scientific subject, and psychological theories therefore need to be supported by evidence-based research. This can explain why more historical forms of psychology, such as the psychodynamic approach developed by Sigmund Freud, are now regarded as unscientific and not falsifiable (i.e. they do not admit the possibility of being shown to be false).

There is compelling evidence for a biological basis for schizophrenia. One explanation may be psychobiology: biological factors inherited from our parents. Evidence suggests that biological factors are implicated in the risk of schizophrenia. Researchers have discovered that the PCM1 gene (Pericentriolar material 1) is implicated in schizophrenia.

It has also been hypothesised that increased levels of the neurotransmitter dopamine can lead to the onset of schizophrenia (Snyder, 1976). The theory was updated by suggesting that high levels of dopamine in the mesolimbic system (the reward system of the brain) are related to positive symptoms, whereas low levels of dopamine in the mesocortic system (the pathway starting from the mid-brain to the pre-frontal cortex) are related to negative symptoms (Brisch, 2014). It has also been found that schizophrenic patients respond well to anti-psychotic medication affecting neurotransmitters.

To determine the genetic basis of behaviour, research investigates twin studies by comparing the agreement between identical and non-identical twins. One study reported a concordance rate of 48% in monozygotic (MZ) twins compared to 17% in dizygotic (DZ) twins (Gottesman & Shield, 1976). This means that schizophrenia is likely to be genetic, as the only difference between MZ twins and DZ twins is how genetically similar they are (MZ share 100% DNA while DZ share 50%).

Despite this evidence-based research supporting a biological cause for schizophrenia, some critics have questioned twin studies. Some researchers have pointed out that environmental factors have a significant impact on learning. The high concordance rates in both MZ and DZ twins perhaps point to the possibility that, given twins share the same environment, schizophrenia is not just genetic but that environmental factors are also involved. Besides, if schizophrenia were entirely genetic, MZ twins would show a 100% concordance rate.

Psychological explanations emphasise how the environment can be critical in the development or relapse of schizophrenia. Theories on family dysfunction indicate that high levels of interpersonal conflict in a family, parents being excessively critical and controlling of their children and difficulties in communication between family members, are sources of stress associated with the development of schizophrenia. Also, according to family socialisation theory (Lidz et al., 1957), schismatic or skewed families fail to provide a stable, supportive environment, as well as appropriate role models for the developing child. This leads to anxiety, and children may develop schizophrenia as a way of handling family conflict.

So, should we look to biological, genetic causes or should we rely on learnt, environmental explanations? The 'nature–nurture' debate comes up in many areas of psychology, but more often than not the question is not so much, 'Is it nature or nurture?' but rather, 'What are the relative contributions of genes and environment, and how do they interact?' The interactionist approach in psychology recognises the importance of the combination of biological and environmental factors for the development of a disorder. In schizophrenia, the diathesis-stress model illustrates that a biological vulnerability (diathesis) interacts with environmental stressors such as stress, to trigger or worsen a schizophrenic episode.

Genetic factors are also associated with faulty dopaminergic systems and abnormal functioning of other neurotransmitters such as serotonin. Genes alone do not cause schizophrenia but instead increase the likelihood that environmental stressors can trigger a schizophrenic episode. Environmental stressors include both psychological and social triggers, such as family dysfunction, substance abuse, critical life events and traumatic experiences, which can cause excessive stress to the individual. So, those usually genetically at risk of developing the disorder will be those most vulnerable to such triggers. Barlow and Durand (2009) found that in a family history of schizophrenics, there was a genetic link but also a dysfunctional stressor that elevated the risk of developing schizophrenia.

With all the good research attempting to explain an important issue such as schizophrenia, how are we to decide which, if any, is correct? One of the strengths of psychology is its capacity to draw on theoretical perspectives derived from different traditions, from biological and medical to philosophical and sociological. The psychologist understands that there are many factors that impact on human behaviour, and sees each of the various explanations as valuable contributions to a complex puzzle. This is why psychology degree courses always cover a number of psychological perspectives in an attempt to explain human behaviour (see 'What is psychology really like to study?' later in this chapter).

Psychological experiments

Landmark social psychology experiments in the 1950s and 1960s banished forever the notion that evil acts could only be committed by evil people. Up until then, people committing outrageous crimes against other people were seen to possess some form of moral or character defect. While it is true that there are a number of dispositional (internal) factors linked to criminal behaviour, what these famous studies showed is that even an ordinary, everyday person could be manipulated into committing an evil act through social influences. Take Stanley Milgram's experiment conducted at Yale University in 1963, for example. By engineering a tightly controlled situation where participants felt compelled to obey the supervising experimenter who was with them, Milgram was able to induce normal, temperate men into electro-shocking another man with volts that were labelled 'danger of death'. It was found that 65% of the participants delivered a potentially fatal shock (350V), with only a few refusing the orders of the researcher and abandoning the experiment. Fortunately, in this case, the man who had supposedly 'died' was an assistant of the experimenter and was only acting. The participants could not see him but, rather, heard his cries from the adjacent room and believed in the reality of the situation.

Some critics suggested that the high level of obedience in this study was because American culture was very authoritarian and obedient in the early 1960s. Therefore, the results found in this study may not reflect obedience nowadays. Another study, by Jerry M. Burger, that was published in American Psychologist (Volume 64, January 2009) partially replicated Milgram's procedures as, firstly, participants were constantly reminded that they could leave the study at any point and keep any money they were offered. Also, participants were informed that the same applied to the confederate and so when they heard the confederate protesting they acknowledged his right to withdraw. Despite these changes, Burger's results were similar to Milgram's study, as 70% of the participants obeyed, and there were no gender differences. To conclude, despite the effects of changes in societal attitudes on human behaviour, the same situation factors that resulted in high levels of obedience in Milgram's study still operate in modern societies. Milgram suggested that people could be manipulated into behaving in ways that they would never normally behave in three different occasions: (i) when they face an ambiguous and uncertain situation that makes them feel tense; (ii) when they switch from being in an autonomous state and having full responsibility for their actions to being in an agentic state where someone else takes responsibility for their actions; and (iii) when they are introduced gradually to a course of actions. Burger finishes his summary of the experiment with a thought-provoking question: if one was able to influence a group of normal, healthy men to commit such acts of violence against their fellow men, how much more would a government, with its infinitely greater power and resources, be able to influence society? Milgram's study has thus given us a profound insight into the nature of atrocities such as the Holocaust.

Many other studies since then have confirmed the power of social influences in directing our behaviour. One that stands out is Philip Zimbardo's prison study at Stanford University. A group of students were recruited to take part in a simulated prison. They were randomly assigned to take the role of either a prisoner or a guard and placed in an area of the university that had been modified to look like a prison. One of the most striking elements of this study was how quickly the people involved took to their respective roles. The simulation was supposed to last for two weeks but had to be abandoned after only six days, as people conformed so strongly to their social roles. Prisoners became distressed, dejected and began to lose a sense of themselves, while several guards became more and more sadistic in their behaviour. Even Zimbardo himself, who had taken the title of Prison Warden as well as being the researcher of the study, began to lose himself in the role.

You may have wondered whether it was right for the participants in these studies to be tricked, upset and humiliated. Such experiments led to professional bodies such as the British Psychological Society (BPS) introducing ethical guidelines for researchers to ensure that participants are treated with respect, so that they are not deceived or harmed in any way and their anonymity is guaranteed. On the other hand, Milgram and Zimbardo got insight into human behaviour in ways that they could not have done otherwise. Understanding the need to weigh up ethical issues against practical considerations is now an important feature of all psychology courses.

Studying psychology will open the doors to a deeper understanding of human behaviour. When we are called upon to explain another person's evil act, many of us might say: 'He is just a bad person.' A student of psychology will pose the question: 'What else might be going on?' Such thoughts will then be developed into specific research questions and hypotheses that can be tested scientifically, for example in experiments, observational studies or surveys.

Scientific methods

Problems with sleep are on the increase. Many people have trouble dropping off to sleep or getting back to sleep if they wake in the middle of the night. Similarly, many people seem to have an explanation and a cure for sleep problems. How are we to determine which, if any, of the myriad explanations for sleep disturbance have validity? Do we have to go through them one by one, while suffering with poor sleep, until we find something that works?

Scientific methods, when applied to psychological issues, provide us with a powerful way of determining those explanations that are valid and those that should be confined to the realms of 'folk' psychology – interesting ideas that lack any true power.

The placebo effect, for example, is one anomaly that can point us in the right direction. This effect shows the power of belief to heal; a person given a sugar pill (medically ineffective) who believes it to be actual medication can recover more rapidly from illness. This shows us that any treatment for a psychological problem must demonstrate its effectiveness over a placebo, or else the treatment is no better than wishful thinking. We can do this by dividing a sample of people with the illness in two, and treating half with the placebo (control group) and half with the actual treatment (experimental group).

In light of this, we can surely separate out explanations for sleep problems into two categories: explanations that have been the subject of a controlled experiment, or explanations that have come about anecdotally from someone who has had a single experience and is passionate about the result. These single case studies can be compelling, but they tell us little about the true effectiveness of a particular explanation.

When it comes to explaining psychological difficulties that you or your friends and family face, do we rely on single cases that we have heard or read about for our explanations, or do we seek explanations that are backed up by good, solid scientific research demonstrating their validity as an explanation? What are the dangers of relying on single case studies, or the drawbacks of relying on lab studies or surveys? A student of psychology learns to combine different research methods, reflecting the complexity and variety of human behaviour.

The rise of neuroscience

Philosophers and psychologists like to debate the difference between mind and brain. One way to think of it is to compare the brain to a computer: the mind is the software while the brain is the hardware. During the last century cognitive psychologists developed ways of studying mental processes through inference from careful observation of responses in lab-based tasks.

In the past few years fMRI (functional magnetic resonance imaging) scanners and PET (positron emission tomography) scans have increasingly been used to map the functions of the brain. Journalists like reporting on the latest advances in neuroscience because this seems more like the layperson's idea of science and the colourful brain-scan images look great in newspapers.

Cognitive neuropsychology is the study of biological structures to explain mental processes through the use of brain scanning methods. Cognitive psychology is concerned with mental processes such as perception, attention, reasoning and memory. For example, 40 years ago, medical case studies and lab experiments led to the proposal of models of working memory, as distinct from long-term memory. Placing someone in a scanner and giving them various memory tests now allows us to see the areas of the brain involved in different aspects of working memory.

However, some psychologists have been critical of the excitement about neuroscience, pointing out that a good deal of research just locates the site of mental functions which we knew must be carried out somewhere in the brain anyway. Either way, neuropsychology is still in its infancy and it is likely that this technological approach will produce more and more insights into the functioning of mind and brain in the future. University courses are increasingly reflecting this in their content and there is more of an emphasis on biology.

The study of individual differences

Are people becoming more or less aggressive? Why does anorexia occur only in some countries? What makes one person more intelligent than another? Why do some people form secure and lasting relationships, while others are married and divorced several times? Society is always asking these questions and psychologists attempt to answer them. For instance, we can devise tests to measure levels of aggression and then manipulate different factors such as the level of violence in a video game to see what effect it might have on people's aggressiveness. Or we could give people questionnaires about their early relationships with their parents during childhood and their attitudes to their current adult romantic relationships that would enable us to look for links between early attachment experiences and adult behaviour.

Taking the example of aggression again, an evolutionary psychologist would be interested in aggression as an inherited human instinct and the adaptive function that it played in the life of our early ancestors, while a social psychologist would ask how present-day social situations make people aggressive.

By contrast, the individual differences approach is interested in measuring the relative aggressiveness of individuals and attempting to identify the factors that account for the differences between them. This approach has been applied for much of the history of psychology to measure intelligence, personality or psychological abnormalities. Most of us will have taken some kind of psychological test at one time or other, maybe an IQ test or a personality test that rates how much of an extrovert or introvert we are.

Psychometric tests are big business, with a number of organisations devoted to producing reliable and valid tests for use in all kinds of settings: in education, prisons, the armed services, the health service or businesses. These tests are all aimed at assessing people's suitability for something: training, a job or some form of treatment perhaps (known as an 'intervention').

However, some psychologists ask whether giving someone a score on a personality scale really tells us much about the uniqueness of that person as an individual. Such researchers might favour a qualitative approach, interviewing people to get an in-depth understanding of their personal worlds. Others have denied that personality is stable or predictable at all, arguing that psychometric tests are too influenced by social desirability or the context in which they are completed. At university you will be able to explore such debates further and if you go on to a career in psychology you are likely to use or even design psychometric tests.

Psychotherapy

Imagine yourself sitting in front of a psychotherapist for the first time. Having struggled for some time with constant self-criticism, depression and intense anxiety that seems to come from nowhere (always at the most inconvenient times), you have finally summoned the courage to ask for help. Fifty years ago, the therapist would most likely have been psychoanalytic, taking their lead from pioneers like Sigmund Freud. Your current struggles would be explained as the result of unresolved conflicts residing deep within your unconscious and it would be the therapist's job to help bring those issues to your awareness, perhaps through hypnosis, dream interpretation or free association, so that you could 'work them through'.

Modern psychological treatments, or 'talking therapies', have developed over the last 30–40 years, focusing on present, conscious thoughts, and have begun what is amounting to a revolution in the field of mental health. Aaron Beck, inventor of Cognitive Behavioural Therapy (CBT), shows us that our immediate thought patterns cause us to interpret the world in systematic ways, sometimes ensnaring us in a tangle of negative or self-defeating thoughts. Such dysfunctional beliefs and thought processes are responsible for negative emotions and maladaptive behaviour. In comparison to traditional psychoanalytic approaches, which can take many years to unravel a person's neuroses, CBT is quick and targets our illogical or dysfunctional thoughts from day one.

Randomised controlled trials (RCTs) have demonstrated that CBT is at least as effective as antidepressant drugs for mild to moderate depression. This is just one area of psychology that not only stands up to scientific scrutiny but also has a profoundly positive impact on the human race as a whole. The CBT approach is used in a number of areas of mental health and has also been adopted by coaching psychologists, who are engaged to improve performance and wellbeing in a range of contexts from sport to business.

While an undergraduate degree will not train you to be a psychotherapist, students who enter postgraduate training in clinical or counselling psychology will learn these skills.

What is psychology really like to study?

Psychology is an increasingly popular subject of study, with 191 higher education institutions in the UK (and 1,260 higher education institutions worldwide) offering degree-level courses in the subject as a free-standing degree programme in its own right, and many more institutions offer psychology courses as modules in other combined programmes. Despite this growth in student places, there are still, however, some popular misconceptions about the content of degree programmes. They do not offer students the chance to spend three years studying the works of Freud. Nor do they enable you to see into other people's innermost thoughts. In particular, a psychology degree does not qualify you to work as a therapist or counsellor.

Psychology is taught as a **scientific** subject and students spend most of their time studying the results of research into human behaviour and theories that are based on experimental findings.

What is it like to study psychology at university?

'I am in my second year of a psychology degree. It is a fascinating programme. Last year we were introduced to topics that we had covered to some extent at A level. For example, I was familiar with some aspects of development, such as cognitive development and the theories of Piaget and Vygotsky. Of course we went into greater depth, but I found it quite easy to follow the lectures and to contribute with comments and questions because I knew how to evaluate key theories, which was part of the A level specification. In the first year, we mainly had lectures to attend every week and assignments to write, which were challenging at the beginning. However, I attended workshops for additional support in writing essays and building arguments in an academic way using scientific language. At A level we learnt how to write psychological reports, which was what the lecturers were expecting us to follow.'

George

'To be honest, I struggled a lot in the first year because I had not taken psychology as an A level. Most students had taken the subject and so they already had some knowledge. I was a bit lost at the beginning, but following the advice of my personal tutor, I studied hard and thoroughly for each module, attended all my lectures and workshops and did a lot of independent learning. I am in my third year now and things are much easier. I study as hard as in the first year, and I have my daily routine of spending my free time at the library reading and preparing for the next lectures, and writing my revision notes so as to be ready for my exams at the end of the term.

'I know students might feel like fish out of water at the beginning, but if they are motivated then they will not struggle. My advice to them would be to ask questions during the lectures and do a lot of independent learning. Having dyslexia, my writing was pretty awful; but because of the amount of reading that I do, my writing has improved dramatically. Also, take part in discussions during the lectures and do not be afraid to make mistakes. It is part of the learning process!'

Tara

'During my Psychology A level, I enjoyed development and research methods the most. I am now in the first year of my degree, and this term we studied Developmental Psychology and covered similar material to the A level syllabus. I could remember animal studies and all the work that was done by Bowlby and Ainsworth. My first assignment was on the implication of early attachment to later relationships, which we had also discussed at A level.

'I was also good at research methods at A level, which proved to be a great advantage, as we started with all the basics in research methods in the first term. For instance, we had an open-book class test where we had to write a hypothesis based on a study: explain if it was one- or two-tailed, what the experimental design was, explain why a specific

> statistical test was used to analyse the data and whether the result was significant. We also have multiple-choice quizzes as part of our assignments (40% of the final grade) and essays to write (60% of the final grade). I think that the most important for me is that I have fun and enjoy my learning.'
>
> Huang
>
> 'Studying Psychology at UCL has been both challenging and incredibly rewarding. The course is rigorous and research-focused, which has pushed me to think critically about how we understand human behaviour. In first year, much of the focus was on building a strong foundation in core areas such as cognitive, biological, developmental and social psychology, alongside research methods and statistics. At first, the statistics and coding elements (especially using R studio) felt intimidating, but over time I've really come to appreciate how essential they are for analysing psychological data and interpreting research accurately.'
>
> Tom

On a degree course you will learn about a great deal of published research and you will also carry out some yourself. Just as psychology embraces a range of theoretical perspectives, it also employs a variety of methodologies, so you are likely to gain experience of different approaches to research such as experiments, observational studies, surveys and interviews.

The examples in the sections above are just an indication of the many different topics you might study for a psychology degree. On a BPS-accredited course you will cover all of the following areas. It is worth mentioning that some universities offer option modules in Year 2 and Year 3 of their academic curriculum, where students can be specialised in certain psychological areas. Some universities also offer a placement year or practical work experience in the UK or abroad. Lastly, in some universities there is also the option to study psychology for a year at a university abroad.

- **Biological psychology:** how the brain influences behaviour, the effects of hormones, how it can be affected by drugs.
- **Cognitive psychology:** how we remember, learn, think, reason, perceive, speak and understand.
- **Developmental psychology:** how humans develop physically, mentally and socially during childhood and adolescence and their lifespan.
- **Social psychology:** how human behaviour and experience are affected by social context such as in groups and relationships.
- **Conceptual and historical issues:** how psychological explanations have changed over time, and key debates that shape the future of psychology.

- **Individual differences:** consider the differences rather than the similarities between people, such as in personality.
- **Research methods:** quantitative and qualitative methods, research design, data collection, analysis and interpretation.
- **Empirical project:** an extensive piece of empirical research to illustrate research skills such as planning, considering and overcoming ethical issues, analysing and synthesising data, and disseminating research findings.

> 'I am so grateful to have taken A level Psychology before starting my university course as it put me in an advantageous position over students who had not studied psychology before. I was familiar with all the major theories and knew most of the research studies that my professors presented in the class; I was also familiar with how to form criticisms based on methodological issues. I was very confident in participating in class discussion because I had already developed a scientific approach in higher education. My previous knowledge also helped me to grasp the concepts of completely new modules and research studies.'
>
> Freya

Why is psychology so popular?

Overall, then, why is psychology such a popular subject for a first degree? There are several reasons.

Potential students are attracted to a subject that gives them insights into human behaviour, and students of psychology need to have a basic interest in other people and themselves.

> 'I was always interested in why people behave the way they do; I think that this was triggered by facing difficulties in my own life, my own demons, and I wanted to understand myself first before being able to understand others.'
>
> Rebecca

> 'I decided to study psychology because I have always been fascinated by how people think, feel and behave. I wanted to understand what drives human actions and emotions, and how psychological principles can be used to improve people's wellbeing. Psychology combines science and empathy, it allows me to explore the mind through evidence-based research while also helping others in practical, meaningful ways. My goal is to become a CBT therapist in the future and be specialised in addiction.'
>
> Chris

It is a particularly attractive subject for mature students, who may already have touched on the subject during previous training. Business managers, nurses and social services staff may well have been introduced to some of the basic concepts in psychology and want to learn more.

Although now classed as a science, psychology is a subject that can be seen to span both arts and science subjects. It attracts students who have broadly based interests and abilities, who do not want to be seen as either an 'arts' or a 'science' person. A background in philosophy or languages can be as relevant as one in biology or mathematics. That said, those with some science background will be at an advantage due to the focus on scientific methods. Do not be put off if you have an arts background though, as enthusiasm for the subject, open-mindedness and willingness to learn new skills are just as important.

> 'I studied psychology, art and drama for A levels. I did not really know whether I wanted to study psychology or arts at university. I was fascinated by psychology but I had realised that I did not want to become a counsellor or a CBT therapist. After speaking with my psychology teacher, he suggested I look at art therapy courses. I had never thought of it before and it was a brilliant idea as I was able to combine my artistic nature with my passion for psychology!'
>
> Emma

Finally, although the subject of psychology has been studied at university level for a century – the first professor of psychology was appointed in 1919 – it is still seen as a comparatively 'new' subject and, because of the volume of research carried out around the world, students will be studying a subject in which the boundaries of knowledge are constantly changing. What is more, as a result of the diverse applications of psychology in, for example, healthcare, sports psychology and organisational development, many new and exciting work opportunities are being created.

2 | Careers in psychology

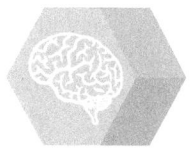

It is important to consider the career you wish to follow after completing your degree, as this may affect the type of psychology course you choose to take. Depending on your own reasons for studying the subject, a psychology degree can be seen as either academic (such as English) or vocational (like medicine).

An accredited degree in psychology can be the first step towards becoming a psychologist, but it will also give you valuable skills that can be used in a variety of sectors. A report by a group of leading psychologists representing the BPS, Advance HE and the Association of Heads of Psychology Departments concluded that an accredited UK undergraduate psychology programme has three main strengths.

1. It covers a wide range of approaches and methodologies, all focused on understanding human behaviour.
2. It provides for great flexibility in choice of future career, in psychology or elsewhere.
3. It develops self-critical ability, creating the motivation and capacity to develop and to meet change.

Psychology graduates are highly regarded by employers and have a good chance of finding employment. This is because the skills they acquire are transferable across many careers. However, over the years the number of psychology graduates has come to vastly outweigh the number of openings for professional psychologists. The latest graduate research from the Higher Education Careers Services Unit (HECSU), 'What do graduates do?' (2025), shows that, 15 months after graduation, 75.8% of psychology graduates were employed (full time, part time or working and studying) – a similar rate to all other social science degrees (education, geography, sociology, politics, law). However, psychology graduates made up the smallest percentage of full-time employees (48.9%) and the fourth lowest percentage of unemployed graduates of the six social science subjects. Specifically 8.6% of psychology graduates were in further study, the third highest percentage across the social science subjects. The relatively high figure of psychology graduates continuing with their studies is an indication of the need to gain further qualifications in order to practise as a psychologist.

There are essentially three main career routes for those who complete a degree course in psychology.

1. To train as a professional psychologist by completing several years of further study and training at postgraduate level.
2. To enter work or postgraduate training that builds on or relates to knowledge gained during a psychology degree programme.
3. To find a graduate-level career which is unrelated to psychology but which may reflect your particular skills and interests.

> For more information about psychology as a career, you should look at the British Psychological Society's website: www.bps.org.uk/career-options-psychology.

The three routes are outlined in more detail below to give you an idea of what you might expect after three or four years of study.

Professional psychology

Statutory regulation for psychologists in the UK was introduced in 2009. Nine specialist titles are now protected by law and regulated by the Health and Care Professions Council (HCPC), which has the responsibility for maintaining a register of practitioner psychologists. The regulated titles are:

- practitioner psychologist;
- registered psychologist;
- clinical psychologist;
- counselling psychologist;
- educational psychologist;
- forensic psychologist;
- health psychologist;
- occupational psychologist;
- sport and exercise psychologist.

Certain professionals refer to themselves as *psychologists*, *counsellors*, *psychotherapists* or *therapists*. These titles are not legally protected, meaning that individuals using them are not required to be registered with the HCPC. As a result, anyone not listed on the HCPC Register is not subject to its regulation.

You cannot practise under one of these specific titles without taking the necessary training and becoming chartered via the BPS. As a rule of thumb, you will need a doctorate level qualification for any of these roles. However, generic titles such as counsellor, psychotherapist or therapist are also used in some other professions, as these are not protected titles.

As an undergraduate on an accredited degree you can join the BPS as a student member and get the monthly members' magazine *The Psychologist*. This publishes employment ads for psychologists, which can give you a good idea of the type of work, the range of employers and the remuneration that can be expected.

Studying for a career in psychology takes on average seven years (including the three or four years for your undergraduate degree), but this can vary depending on your academic profile to date and the type of psychology you want to practise. If you wish to be a professional psychologist you must ensure that your degree will give you the Graduate Basis for Chartered Membership (GBC) of the BPS. This is normally gained by following a course that is accredited by the Society. Not all undergraduate and postgraduate courses are accredited by the BPS, and you will need accreditation if you wish to become a Chartered Psychologist. To check if your selected course is a BPS-accredited course, visit https://portal.bps.org.uk/Accredited-Courses. If you do take a course that is not accredited or you are changing career it is possible to take a conversion course that will enable you to move on to the postgraduate training.

Once they have gained accreditation, graduates will then have to start on a sometimes lengthy period of postgraduate study and practical experience to qualify for chartered status to enable them to practise professionally. There is often intense competition for places on postgraduate courses. For example, according to the Clearing House for Postgraduate Courses in Clinical Psychology, only one in five applicants for clinical psychology courses was successful in 2025. There are 1,142 BPS-accredited undergraduate degree courses and 241 postgraduate courses in the UK. The main professional career routes are described below and illustrated in Figure 1 (overleaf).

Assistant psychologist

One way to achieve a Chartered Psychologist membership is to initially become an assistant psychologist. Students who have finished their undergraduate studies and want to gain clinical experience in their chosen field tend to follow this pathway. This is a great opportunity to work in the clinical, healthcare and non-profit field under the supervision of an experienced clinician, while being part of a dedicated multi-disciplinary team. As these positions are highly competitive, students with a postgraduate degree may have a higher chance of being selected.

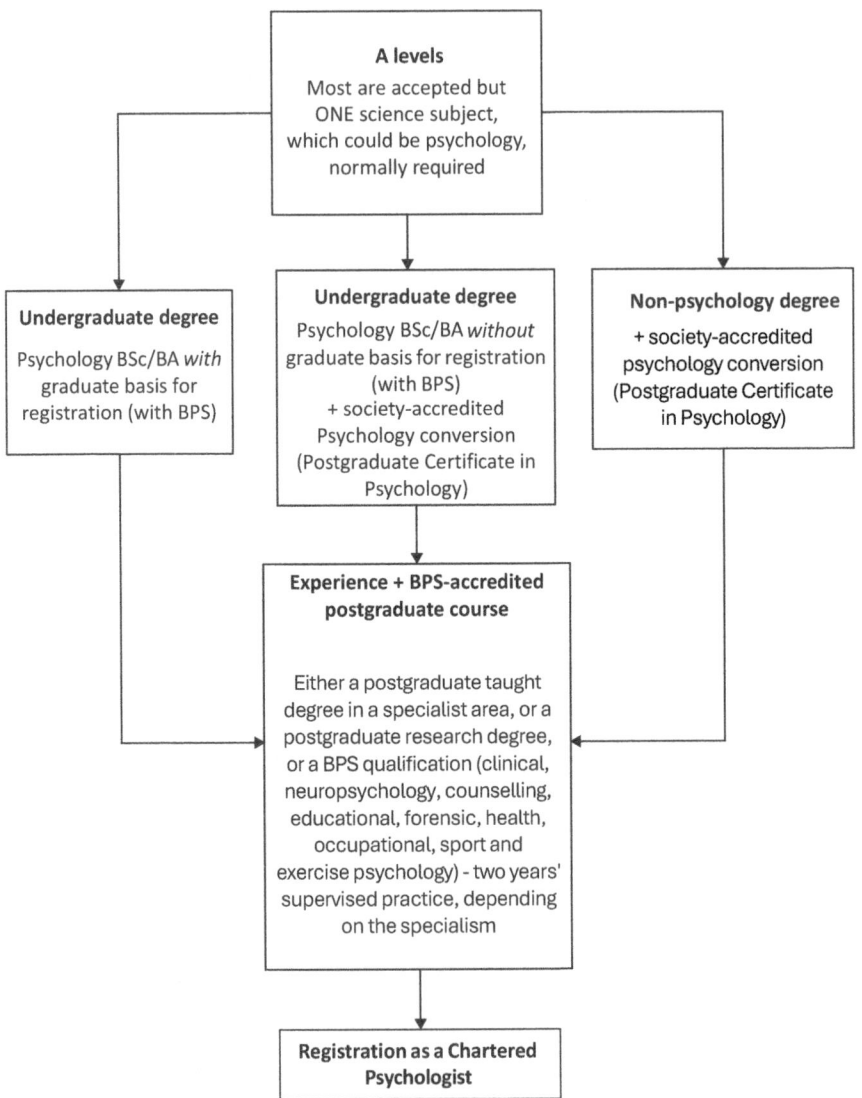

Figure 1: Routes to becoming a Chartered Psychologist

Clinical Associate in Psychology (England) and Clinical Associate in Applied Psychology (Scotland)

This is a specialist mental health professional who is responsible for assessing, formulating and treating clients within a specified range of conditions and age, either in primary care, adult mental health settings or institutions that care for children, young people and their families. Unlike clinical psychologists, clinical associates work within certain specialised areas under the supervision of a fully qualified practitioner psychologist.

Clinical psychology

This is the largest specialism in professional psychology, and clinical psychologists work mainly in the National Health Service (NHS), Child and Adolescent Mental Health Services (CAMHS) and social services and in private practice. They work alongside other professionals and with clients of all ages to assess their needs, provide therapy and carry out research into the effects of different therapeutic methods. Their clients may be otherwise normal people who may have one of a range of problems such as drug dependency, emotional and interpersonal problems or particular learning difficulties. The clinical psychologist role should not be confused with that of the psychiatrist.

Entry to training programmes is highly competitive and you will need a good class in your degree (a 2.i or above) as well as relevant work experience, following the GBC. This can be of two kinds – either work experience in some aspect of clinical care or community work, or experience as an assistant psychologist or a psychological wellbeing practitioner working alongside existing clinical psychologists in a health authority. Vacancies for assistants occur quite frequently, but after working in this role there is no guarantee that you will gain entry to a professional training programme, which takes a further three years and leads to a doctoral degree. This final stage of professional training can take the form of either full-time study at a university coupled with practical experience or an in-service training programme with a health authority. Clinical psychologists require an accredited degree and chartered membership and an accredited doctorate in clinical psychology.

> 'I have just finished my Psychology BSc and am now applying for a postgraduate course. I would like to get a specialisation in anxiety disorders, and have found a university with a team that specialises in this field. My goal is to become a clinical psychologist, but I know that I have to build my career step by step. While I was doing my

degree, I worked with a clinical team at university that was affiliated to a hospital. I assisted clinical psychologists in their research and could see how demanding their work is at first-hand. Clinical psychologists assess patients on a daily basis and offer tailored treatments to them. Having experience in clinical settings really helps with getting onto a postgraduate course. However, there are so many different routes one could follow. Many of my classmates are looking for careers in sport, occupational and educational psychology. You could work at the Human Resources department of a corporation as an occupational psychologist, at a sports club as a sport psychologist, at a police station as a forensic psychologist or in a school setting as a psychology teacher or a special education needs coordinator. Once you get onto a course, you can then decide which route you would like to follow, as a huge range of modules are covered. I only decided what I wanted to do during my last year. It was definitely an intriguing journey.'

Anna

Counselling psychology

A counselling psychologist combines psychological theory and research with therapeutic practice to help people to deal with psychological problems. Typically, these might include bereavement and loss, or relationship and family problems. The counselling psychologist usually works on a one-to-one basis with the client and helps them develop strategies to deal with life problems. Counselling psychologists work in a wide range of settings: hospitals and health centres, community mental health teams or child and adult mental health services, as well as in private practice, industry, education or business. To attain chartered status as a counselling psychologist, an accredited doctoral course or a BPS qualification in counselling psychology is required, following the GBC.

Educational psychology

Educational psychologists are experts in child and adolescent development. They work mainly for local education authorities, although you will find a need for educational psychologists in schools, colleges, nurseries and special units. The role of educational psychologists is to liaise with teachers and parents in identifying and assessing pupils and students with challenges such as learning difficulties, social and emotional problems, disability issues and complex developmental disorders. These can range from dyslexia, to depression, to disruptive classroom behaviour. Educational psychologists use observation, interviews and assessment tests to diagnose problems so they can offer consultation, advice and support to teachers, parents and the young people themselves. Their work and research can also be used to provide training to those working closely with children such as teachers, learning support assistants and teaching assistants. They also provide psychological expertise and training for teachers and others working with children. The referral of children with special educational needs to special schools is a typical example of a situation in which an educational psychologist's advice would be sought.

This specialism requires a lengthy period of further study, training and experience. In England and Wales psychology graduates are required to have some experience of working with children or young people before starting a doctoral course in educational psychology. Examples of the kind of work experience required include teaching, social work, speech and language therapy or working as an assistant psychologist or a special educational needs coordinator in an educational psychology service. The formal training is then followed by one year of supervised practice. The University of Cardiff and Queen's University Belfast now operate their own admissions process so it is worth contacting the universities directly. In Scotland, educational psychologists operate their own admissions process; only the University of Dundee provides this training including a two-year MSc in Educational Psychology followed by a one-year supervised probationary period. Supervision is provided by Chartered Psychologists who are members of the Scottish Division of Educational Psychology. Upon successful completion, the Professional Doctorate in Educational Psychology is awarded. For more information visit: https://www.dundee.ac.uk/postgraduate/applied-educational-psychology

Forensic psychology

Also known as criminal psychologists, people in this professional group work mainly in the prison service, although they might also work in secure hospitals, social services or in private consultancy with the police services. For the most part, a forensic psychologist's role is to modify offender behaviour, respond to the changing needs of staff and prisoners, along with reducing stress for staff and prisoners. A key part of their work is the assessment of prisoners in terms of their rehabilitation needs and their level of risk, based on psychometric test results and clinical interviews. In addition, forensic psychologists carry out research and put in place treatment programmes to change offending behaviour and often work with groups of offenders to achieve this aim. In addition, some carry out research to provide evidence for practice, undertake statistical analysis for offender profiling, give evidence in court to provide an expert view, and advise on parole boards. TV crime programmes and books have raised public awareness of offender profiling as an area that some forensic psychologists specialise in, but in reality only a few psychologists actually work in this area and its use remains controversial.

You would need a doctorate, or a master's degree plus two years' practice through an HCPC-approved programme, for the BPS qualification in forensic psychology.

Health psychology

Working in a variety of settings – such as hospitals, community health, health research units and public health departments – health psychologists look at the links between healthcare and illness, using psychological knowledge to promote wellbeing and an understanding of physical illness. This can include helping people with behaviours that entail a health risk (such as smoking or drug use); preventative measures (exercise, diet, health checks); the delivery of healthcare; and the psychological aspects of illness, such as how patients cope with pain or terminal illness. They might advise doctors on the best ways to communicate with their patients and ensure that they follow the treatment prescribed for them. Health psychologists also work on promoting healthy lifestyles and may be called upon to deal with problems identified by NHS trusts.

There are a number of accredited MSc courses for candidates who have achieved the GBC. Following this, candidates must gain a Qualification in Health Psychology Stage 2 (QHP Stage 2) or a BPS-accredited doctorate in Health Psychology. In Scotland, an NHS-funded Stage 2 training scheme operates to employ trainee health psychologists.

Neuropsychology

Neuropsychologists work with people of all ages with neurological problems, which might include traumatic brain injury, stroke, toxic and metabolic disorders, tumours and neurodegenerative diseases. Neuropsychologists require not only general clinical skills and knowledge of the broad range of mental health problems, but also a substantial amount of specialist knowledge in the neurosciences. Although this is not a regulated title, a neuropsychologist needs first to be chartered as a clinical or educational psychologist before specialising and receiving further training. The BPS offers a two-year qualification course in Clinical Neuropsychology (QiCN), which leads to a full membership of the Division of Neuropsychology (DoN) and entry to the Society's Specialist Register of Clinical Neuropsychologists.

Occupational psychology

Occupational psychologists are concerned with the behaviour of people at work. Their aim is to increase the effectiveness of the organisation and improve job satisfaction of employees. The specialty of occupational psychology is broader and less formalised than many areas of psychology and touches upon diverse fields such as personnel management and research.

Occupational psychologists can be employed in a variety of roles for a range of employers. They may be employed directly by government departments, public service organisations or big corporations, or they may carry out projects under contract, either as employees of management consultancies engaged by organisations or as freelancers. Other areas of work include the Ministry of Defence, Her Majesty's Prison Service or as trade union representatives or a role in Human Resources. They may also work for companies that specialise in creating and developing psychometric tests for use in recruitment and training.

Within organisations, occupational psychologists may advise senior management on bringing in an organisational change programme, or they might be supporting the HR director in developing staff training or job design, running stress-management workshops or launching a staff attitudes survey. Occupational psychologists often advise on the tests and exercises that might be used for staff recruitment as well. They could find themselves working alongside IT professionals on the design of the interface between equipment and its potential users, or the development of computer systems. To qualify for chartered status in this field, psychology graduates need to complete a specialist master's course. Following this, candidates must gain a Qualification in Occupational Psychology Stage 2 (QHP Stage 2), which involves two years of supervised practice (doctorate level).

Psychological Wellbeing Practitioner (PWP)

Psychological Wellbeing Practitioners (PWPs) are trained to provide psychological assessments and treatments for people who suffer from common mental health problems such as anxiety and depression. In England, they work in NHS Improving Access to Psychological Therapies (IAPT) services for mental health difficulties such as depression and anxiety, and provide a range of low-intensity, evidence-based interventions following a step-by-step care programme. A degree in psychology is not required to get onto a PWP training programme.

Sports and exercise psychology

Sports psychology is a growing field. Increasingly, professional sportsmen and women are using psychologists to help them to improve their performance. Many football clubs, for instance, now employ sports psychologists to work with their players on an individual and team basis. The aim of the sports psychologist is to enhance performance by improving the focus or the motivation of the participants, and to encourage a 'will to win'. They may also help referees to deal with the stressful aspects of their roles, advise coaches on techniques to build cohesion within a squad or among athletes, or support athletes dealing with the psychological consequences of injury. Sports psychologists can be involved in teaching or research or have a private consultancy for treating amateur or elite sportspeople.

To become a Chartered Sports Psychologist you need to have a master's degree plus Stage 2 (doctorate equivalent) of the BPS qualification in sport and exercise psychology or a BPS-accredited doctorate in this field. Should you wish to follow a career in sport psychology, you may find that coaching, fitness and exercise instruction and PE teaching will be advantageous experience and preparation.

Psychologists in teaching, lecturing and research

Academic staff in universities and colleges of higher education will combine teaching activities, such as delivering lectures and running seminars and tutorials, with a commitment to carrying out research. Their task is to keep up to date with the latest research findings in their particular area of expertise. They will spend a considerable amount of time making applications for research funding and, once the research is completed, writing journal articles to publish their findings. Entry to academic posts in psychology is very competitive. Lecturers in higher education are not required to have a teaching qualification but those applying for lecturing posts will be expected to have a PhD and to have some published research. Lecturing posts in psychology may also arise in colleges of further education.

According to data from 'What do graduates do?' (2025), about 7.4% of psychology graduates go on to work in education professions and 20.4% in childcare, health and education professions. Psychology graduates who want to teach in secondary schools should note that psychology is offered at Key Stage 4 and 5 only (GCSE and A level). According to the British Psychological Society, the number of students taking psychology at A level has increased in recent years, creating a demand for qualified psychology teachers. For many years, a shortage of qualified psychology teachers has been problematic for schools and colleges but with universities now offering PGCE courses in psychology, getting into teaching is becoming increasingly accessible. In addition, psychologists can gain the qualified teacher status (QTS) through the assessment-only route if they have taught at two different schools for more than two years (www.gov.uk/government/publications/the-assessment-only-route-to-qts).

Other psychologist roles

There are a number of careers directly involving psychology that do not have titles regulated by the HCPC, several of which are in new and exciting fields for psychologists. People in these occupations may or may not have the title of psychologist but they would all expect to use psychological theories and methods in their work. Examples of a few of these are psychological wellbeing practitioner, assistant psychologist and clinical associate in applied psychology. Further examples are explained in detail below.

AI behavioural science/Psychology + AI/ Computational psychology

This emerging area combines psychology, data science and artificial intelligence (AI) to understand, predict and influence human behaviour. It focuses on how people interact with technology and how psychological principles can guide the design of intelligent systems. Professionals in this field study human thought processes, decision making and emotional responses using large-scale digital data (e.g. social media, wearable devices, apps). They then use AI tools like machine learning and predictive analytics to identify patterns in behaviour.

Animal psychology

A number of psychology first degrees now include options in animal behaviour, reflecting the growth of research in this area. Animal psychologists might work in agriculture, advising on the management and welfare of farm animals, or they might work as pet therapists alongside vets, advising people on their animals' problem behaviour and helping to retrain them. If you are hoping to work in animal training or welfare, it might be more important to study for a degree that specifically covers animal behaviour, or joint honours with zoology, even if the degree itself is not BPS-accredited. There are also specialist postgraduate courses in animal behaviour therapy. According to Advance HE, there could be opportunities to work in zoos, laboratories, wildlife offices, eco-tourism, animal welfare charities or government departments such as the Department for Environment, Food and Rural Affairs (DEFRA), although many animal behaviourists are probably freelance.

Child Wellbeing Practitioner (CWP)

Children's Wellbeing Practitioners (CWPs) are trained to deliver guided self-help to children, young people and families experiencing mild to moderate difficulties such as anxiety, low mood or common behavioural issues. They can work across a range of settings, including Child and Adolescent Mental Health Services (CAMHS), local authorities and voluntary organisations. Their role can involve carrying out assessments, providing one-to-one or telephone support, running workshops or group sessions and involving service users in different activities. Those training to become CWPs complete a one-year postgraduate certificate programme, currently offered by University College London (UCL) or King's College London (KCL), alongside practical work within a service. During training, CWPs learn to provide short-term, evidence-based interventions designed to offer low-intensity psychological support. This includes helping young people with mild to moderate anxiety (in both primary and secondary school), low mood (particularly among adolescents) and behavioural challenges (by working with parents of children under eight years old). Each service has set their own criteria for assessing applications but generally at least a second-class Bachelor's degree from a UK university or an overseas equivalent in a relevant subject is required to be eligible for the training.

Coaching psychology

Coaching has been defined by Myles Downey (author of *Effective Coaching*) as 'the art of facilitating the performance, learning and development of another'. Coaches use a range of psychological theories and approaches that are closely related to counselling but they work with people to help them tackle practical problems in their personal or professional lives and achieve their goals. Within organisations, coaches may be hired to work one-to-one with employees to help improve performance in a job, to provide stress-management training or to improve personal organisation skills. As with therapists, coaches may come from various backgrounds outside psychology, such as management; there is, therefore, no accredited route. Many coaches are self-employed.

Consumer and marketing psychology

Marketing as a business discipline owed much of its early development to psychology, being involved as it is with understanding consumer behaviour. There are good opportunities for psychology graduates in market research, which demands both quantitative and qualitative skills. Projects might include advising on product design, creating brands or studying customer lifestyles. Consumer and marketing psychologists might be employed by a big market research firm, or by a consultancy or work freelance. There is no postgraduate requirement but a joint degree, such as psychology and marketing or psychology and business, would be an advantage, plus relevant work experience.

Cyberpsychology

Otherwise known as human–computer interaction (HCI), this is an exciting and rapidly growing field that overlaps with computer science and organisational psychology. The possible roles are very varied. It can involve studying and advising on human interactions with all types of electronic technology, from games to smartphones, to aircraft consoles, to business software. Psychological techniques such as eye-tracking or behavioural analysis are used to understand the experience and satisfaction of users of technology ('user experience field') so as to help design user-friendly products. Another area is e-learning, where roles might involve developing online tools to support teaching programmes. HCI is also involved in mental health, from researching how to prevent or treat computer addiction to the use of video games and simulations to treat mental health problems. A postgraduate qualification would be an advantage here, especially as you could be in competition with graduates from related disciplines, but most important would be the ability to match your attributes and skills to the particular role.

Educational Mental Health Practitioner (EMHP)

Education Mental Health Practitioners (EMHPs) work within both educational and healthcare environments to deliver early mental health interventions for children and young people in schools and colleges. These positions are part of the government's initiative to expand access to mental health and wellbeing support. Trainee EMHPs complete a 12-month, full-time training programme that combines university-based learning with supervised practical experience. This enables them to develop the knowledge and skills needed to work effectively across both education and mental health settings. The training is funded at the equivalent of NHS Band 4, and trainees earn postgraduate-level academic credits. Upon successful completion, they qualify as EMHPs and are guaranteed employment within a Mental Health Support Team (MHST) working in educational environments. Entry criteria differ between universities, but applicants must be able to study at degree level and have previous relevant learning or qualifications in areas such as child development, wellbeing or mental health. Prior experience working with children or young people, along with a strong understanding of the English education system, is also highly valued.

Engineering psychology

Engineering psychologists are interested in the relationship between human beings and machines. This field, also known as human factors engineering, explores how products and technologies on the market affect human everyday life experiences. Engineering psychology is expanding fast due to the rapid advances in technology, consumerism and a high demand for new products. Apart from analysing human interactions with the use of products, they collect feedback from consumers and design new products that serve human needs and resolve real-life problems. For instance, engineering psychologists may design new medical tools and operating-room layouts to eliminate medical accidents and errors, or new software programs for head-mounted devices to help patients overcome different forms of anxiety through virtual-reality exposure therapy. They have also developed products such as mobile phones, GPS systems, medical equipment, military equipment, traffic systems and vehicle safety systems. They can be specialised in different fields, such as aerospace, virtual reality, education and training, healthcare, human performance enhancement, product research and workplace safety.

Environmental psychology

Environmental psychologists are interested in the relationships between people and their surroundings. They study how we are affected cognitively and emotionally by the places where we live, work, shop and relax and how we behave in response to different types of environment. They are also involved in looking at the interaction between humans and natural resources and the related area of sustainability behaviour (e.g. recycling or reduction of fossil fuel use). A good master's degree would be a precursor to working in central or local government, or within a consultancy advising architects, planners and engineers.

Parapsychology

According to the Koestler Parapsychology Unit, parapsychology is the study of apparent new means of communication, or exchange of influence, between organisms and environment. Other definitions define parapsychology as the scientific study of psychic phenomena. Keen to show credibility in their field of research, parapsychologists' focus lies in collecting empirical data through laboratory and case studies. They study a variety of different phenomena including extra-sensory perception (ESP), psychokinesis (PK), near death and out-of-body experiences, psychic healing and communication through mediums. Psychic research can be traced back to the nineteenth century, attracting scientists, scholars and philosophers. However, not all scientists accept parapsychology as a legitimate science but consider it a pseudoscience due to its failure to produce conclusive evidence.

To work successfully in this field you must be open-minded and resilient due to the criticism of the field as cases of fraud have been uncovered in some famous studies. For those of you interested in pursuing a career in parapsychology, it is worth noting that it is a small and select field and a job is more likely to be found in universities conducting research or with a private research facility. Some individuals have made successful careers working alone, carrying out their own research and publishing their findings in books and on radio programmes.

Roles in psychology not involving a psychology degree

It is important to distinguish between the role of the psychologist and other professionals carrying out related work in mental health. As you will see, a psychology degree is not a precursor for these other roles but the training is at least as rigorous.

- **Psychiatrist.** A medically trained doctor who chooses to specialise in mental health by taking the membership examinations of the Royal College of Psychiatry. As a consequence of their medical training, psychiatrists can prescribe drug treatments. They will often work as part of a team with clinical psychologists.
- **Psychotherapist or counsellor.** Works with both individuals and groups to provide long-term therapy. They will often encourage clients to reflect on their past experience and early development. In theory, graduates of any subject can become a psychotherapist by taking a three- or four-year training programme of supervised clinical practice and seminars and undergoing personal therapy ('supervision'). For more information see the website of the British Association for Counselling and Psychotherapy: www.bacp.co.uk.

Case study

Rui studied psychology at degree level because he was fascinated by the subject but didn't know what he wanted to do in the future.

'Psychology was definitely the one subject that I put all my effort into during A levels. My psychology teacher's passion and enthusiasm made me realise the significance of this discipline. I got an A* in Psychology, and although I did not achieve the required A*AA for the psychology course, the university accepted me with a lower offer thanks to the A*. The three-year course was amazing and I learnt so much. I was fascinated by anything biological and how drug treatments can influence mental processes. After my final year, I decided to apply to the medical school in order to follow the medical route to become a psychiatrist. Best decision ever.'

Other psychology-related careers

There are several occupations for which a first degree in psychology is a useful entry qualification because of the particular knowledge or skills it provides. For example, an understanding of individual behaviour and social development is highly relevant to careers in teaching and social work. The study of statistical methods and the analysis and interpretation of statistical results can be useful in business and management, especially when devising questionnaires or examining the results of surveys. Any insights that psychology students gain into the nature of individual ability and aptitudes, and the ways these can be measured, will provide a foundation for a career in the assessment and selection of personnel. Knowledge you may acquire about physiological and cognitive psychology can be applied in ergonomics, or human factors design, as it is sometimes called. Yet again, an interest in other people's behaviour or personality may well provide the basis of careers that require an element of pastoral care or interpersonal helping, such as teaching, nursing, management or a religious calling.

As the 'What do graduates do?' survey of 2025's psychology graduates indicates, 12.5% entered legal, social and welfare professions, 11.6% worked as clerical, secretarial and numerical clerks, 9.5% worked as business, human resources and finance officers, 10.7% became health professionals and 4.5% pursued work in marketing, PR and sales. Other psychology graduates pursued options in advertising, IT, engineering or arts, design, culture and sports.

> '*My psychology degree has been incredibly valuable in my marketing career. Studying psychology taught me how to understand human behaviour, what motivates people, how they make decisions and how emotions influence their choices. This insight directly applies to understanding consumer behaviour and creating effective marketing strategies. Research methods and statistics have also been useful, as they help me analyse data, interpret trends and evaluate campaign performance objectively. Modules on social and cognitive psychology strengthened my understanding of persuasion, attention and memory, all crucial for designing impactful adverts and messages. Beyond academics, university projects helped me develop teamwork, communication and critical thinking skills, which are essential for collaborating with colleagues and presenting ideas confidently. Overall, my psychology background has given me both the analytical and interpersonal skills that make marketing not just about selling products, but about understanding people.*'
>
> *Jennifer*

Transferable skills

Many graduates in psychology will choose not to apply the specific knowledge of psychology they have gained from their degree course but, instead, will use the skills that they have gained in a wide range of other graduate-level careers. Indeed these skills are highly regarded by employers. There are graduate job vacancies in the UK that are not subject specific. With a degree in psychology, therefore, it is quite possible to train as an accountant or a solicitor, enter general management, become a journalist or work in information technology. Much will depend on your particular interests and the skills you have developed. In studying psychology, students are often surprised by the number of different skills they develop and which they can use in their work after graduating.

- **Information-seeking and research skills**: the ability to search databases and employ experimental methods.
- **Analytical skills**: the ability to think critically and weigh the evidence from different research findings.
- **Numeracy**: the ability to interpret statistical data and to assess the reliability of experimental results.
- **IT skills**: the ability to use software packages for data analysis and psychological measurement.

These are in addition to the skills that most higher education students will acquire, such as the written communication skills developed in essay and report writing, or the verbal communication skills used in group projects or seminar discussions and making presentations. As you can see, a psychology degree programme may help you to develop a broad range of skills that you can apply in the workplace, but you may need to make this apparent to potential employers.

Case study

Dr Philippa East is a clinical psychologist who runs her own independent practice in Sleaford, Lincolnshire. Philippa has been a Chartered Psychologist for 10 years.

'I originally studied psychology and philosophy as an undergraduate. At university, I was a student welfare rep and worked for the student Nightline. Over the summer after graduating, I did some volunteer work in the field of mental health, with odd jobs with local charities and services. I then was lucky enough to get a job as an assistant psychologist in an adult NHS Eating Disorder Service. In general, it's common for graduates to spend two to three years getting experience in the field of mental health (through volunteering, assistant jobs, research or further study) before applying for clinical training. I then got a place to train as a clinical psychologist at the Institute of Psychiatry. Clinical psychology training is a three-year doctoral programme combining lectures, research and clinical placements.

'After graduating as a clinical psychologist, I took up a job in a community mental health team, and then in a specialist psychosis service in South London. I later worked for the Maudsley Eating Disorders Service, before relocating to Lincolnshire where I worked in the NHS Adult Psychology Service. In 2015, I decided to move from the NHS into the independent sector, and I now run my own therapy practice. Along the way, I've trained in a variety of therapies, including CBT, cognitive analytic therapy and EMDR (Eye Movement Desensitisation and Reprocessing). As a clinical psychologist, I've also been involved in teaching, training and supervising colleagues, carrying out research and consulting to services and teams.

'In a typical day (or week), my main role currently is as a therapist, seeing clients at the practice for their regular therapy sessions. I usually see between four and six clients a day (for an hour's session each). My clients have a range of difficulties, from OCD to depression, eating disorders to work stress. I also have time during the week for admin and liaison. This might mean responding to phone or email enquiries from clients who are thinking about starting therapy, or liaising with a current client's GP who might also be supporting them. On some weeks, I might have a supervision session with the counsellor I supervise, going through his own caseload and supporting him in his own therapy work.

'Once a month I also attend my own supervision, where I talk through my cases with my colleagues, particularly any I am feeling stuck with. In between this, I might have some time to read up on latest research (e.g. in psychology magazines and journals) so that I am keeping abreast of developments in my field. However, the role of a clinical psychologist can be very varied, depending on the job and settings, and might also include conducting research, attending team meetings with other mental health staff such as social workers and psychiatrists or delivering training and teaching.'

Case study

Dimi studied maths, chemistry, biology and psychology at A level. His parents wanted him to become a medical doctor because of the prestige and the financial stability of the profession.

'Throughout my academic journey, excelling in all four subjects was driven by familial expectations, but I did find genuine fascination within the realm of science. While I enjoyed unravelling the mysteries of biology and chemistry and their intricate relationships, it was the complexities of the human mind that truly captivated me. Opting for psychology as my major felt like a natural progression – it was an avenue where I could delve deeper into understanding human behaviour, motivations and the intricate workings of the mind.

'Securing my first-choice university course opened doors to a fulfilling career in forensic psychology. My academic foundations in various scientific disciplines have proved useful to this role – the job demands an interdisciplinary approach, often necessitating an understanding of biological underpinnings, chemical influences and statistical analysis to comprehend and address the complexities of human behaviour within legal contexts.

'Having cultivated a robust background in these scientific domains has not only enriched my professional responsibilities but also provided a holistic perspective that enables me to navigate the multifaceted challenges inherent in forensic psychology. It's immensely gratifying to see how my passion for the human mind has seamlessly merged with my aptitude in these scientific disciplines, allowing me to contribute meaningfully to the field while continuously expanding my understanding of human behaviour.'

3 | Work experience

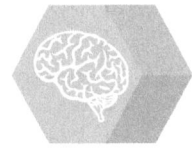

Psychology-related work experience is important to you both in terms of your university application and on a personal level. It has the potential to make your UCAS personal statement stand out from other applicants' and it will give you something to talk about if you are called for an interview. It will also provide you with a better sense of what it would be like to work in fields related to psychology. This is valuable in itself and it will also enable you to make a more informed judgement about the kind of modules you would like to study during your degree and, in turn, about what career you might like to pursue.

Choosing the right kind of work experience

There is a good chance that you will have the same grade profile and a similarly good reference as many other applicants for the same course. This can make it hard for admissions tutors to discriminate between applicants. For this reason, it is important to not only engage in work experience, but to consider how this work experience fits into your long-term plans. Getting the right kind of work experience will really help you to advertise your credentials to admissions tutors as a strong applicant.

> 'It is not necessary to study psychology at A level to apply for a psychology degree course. I was told that my application would be at a disadvantage, but in my personal statement I clearly justified how my subjects – biology, chemistry and sociology – were related to psychology. I also completed an EPQ in the investigation of neural correlates in the development of schizophrenia, where I tried to unravel the complex links between brain abnormalities, neurotransmitters, dysfunctional thought processes and psychotic symptoms. I also volunteered with a local charity and assisted in the delivery of psychoeducational interventions in a disadvantaged group of primary school children. In these ways, I demonstrated that I was academically and professionally engaged with psychology.'
>
> Scott

As we saw in Chapter 2, there are numerous career paths in psychology. If you have an idea about what kind of field you would like to work in after your degree this can help you tremendously when deciding what kind of work experience you would like to engage in. For example, if you want to work as a forensic psychologist, then work experience within the prison service would be better than work experience within a hospital or psychiatric practice. Alternatively, if you want to work as a clinical or counselling psychologist, then work experience within a medical environment such as a hospital or a mental health organisation would be ideal. Table 1 (overleaf) will point you in the right direction.

Making the most of your work experience

Before we move on to considering when and how to arrange work experience it is important for you to have a clear idea of how to conduct yourself when you are at your placement. Companies often take students on work experience so that they can have access to some free labour during the summer months. They get students to photocopy, file, shred paper and make the tea. There is a very good chance that these will be the kinds of tasks you will be given during your work experience. You should expect this to be the case and take on the tasks with a sense of eagerness. Of course, you will not be limited to these responsibilities, and once you have shown that you can be trusted and you are eager to learn, they may give you more duties. It is important to remember that regardless of the task you have to complete, you will be constantly demonstrating traits of your character and your work ethic. There is a massive difference between a volunteer who has finished what they were asked to do and then sits in the office doing nothing and the volunteer who is checking with the manager if there is something else they can help with. At the end of your work experience, you will be asking your employer for a reference and they will address all these important details.

It is also important to acknowledge that many jobs within psychology-related fields have issues related to patient confidentiality. This means that you will not necessarily get to see the kind of nitty-gritty that you might like to see. For these reasons it is very important that you are proactive during your work experience. There is nothing wrong with asking questions – and this is exactly what you should do. Ask them why they do the things they do in this order, or using that mechanism. Ask them why they have this policy rather than that policy.

Perhaps most importantly, try not to get left on your own during tea breaks and lunchtime. These are the times when employees will be able to have a more in-depth chat with you about their roles and what it is like to work in this field. It may even be a good idea to take a notepad and a pencil with you so that you can take notes. These notes

Table 1 Possible work experience opportunities related to psychology

Career area	Possible work experience opportunities
Academic teaching and research	Lecturing and working as a researchers at universities, colleges and schools. In schools, perhaps as a psychology teacher or mentor for younger students. You may also find work experience in research units, such as the MRC Cognition and Brain Sciences Unit in Cambridge.
Assistant psychologist	NHS and the healthcare system. You may also find some work in human resources, education, forensic settings and the non-profit sector.
Clinical Associate in (Applied) Psychology	Specialised primary care and adult mental health settings. You may work with specific types of children, young people and their families to address specific difficulties.
Clinical psychology	Health and social care settings, including hospitals, health centres, community mental health teams, Child and Adolescent Mental Health Services (CAMHS) and social services. Most clinical psychologists are employed by the NHS, but some work in private practice. You might also want to contact the Clearing House for Postgraduate Courses in Clinical Psychology. It typically deals with postgraduates but its handbook gives information about what sort of work experience is desirable, so this may provide you with a lead.
Counselling psychology	Hospitals (acute admissions, psychiatric intensive care, rehabilitation), health centres, NHS IAPT services for mental health disorders such as Anxiety and Depression teams, Community Mental Health teams and CAMHS. Psychologists also tend to work in private practice or in commerce.
Educational psychology	Local education authorities employ the majority of educational psychologists. They work in schools, colleges, nurseries and special units, primarily with teachers and parents. A growing number work as independent or private consultants. Try making contact with the Head of Learning Support at a local school or college and/or with educational psychologists, speech and language therapists, care workers or early years workers in your area. Also, due to their research background, they are often placed within the education authority to conduct research in this field.
Forensic psychology	HM Prison Service should be your starting point. Forensic psychologists are also employed by rehabilitation units, secure hospitals, the social services and in university departments. Some practitioners also go into private consultancy, so direct contact with a forensic psychologist may lead to some form of work-shadowing with them in this capacity. Universities offering the accredited Master's in Forensic Psychology will place their students on work experience, so talking to a tutor on one of these courses could also help.

(Continued)

Table 1 (Continued)

Career area	Possible work experience opportunities
Health psychology	Hospitals, community health settings, academic health research units, health authorities, university departments, local authorities and also consultancy practices. You may get information about local health psychologists from your GP surgery or rehabilitation units in your local area. Universities offering the accredited Master's in Health Psychology will place their students on work experience, so talking to a tutor on one of these courses could also help.
Neuropsychology	Work is mainly in acute settings, regional neuroscience and rehabilitation centres to provide assessments, training and support to brain injury patients and those with neurological problems. Many senior neuropsychologists substantially supplement their income by undertaking private medico-legal consultancy as expert witnesses in personal injury cases, so direct contact with a neuropsychologist could lead to some form of work-shadowing with them in this capacity.
Occupational psychology	Due to its nature, occupational psychologists work in many fields across all sectors. They tend to work in governmental and public services. The civil service is one of the largest single employers of occupational psychologists. The Prison Service, the Home Office, the Employment Department Group (including the Employment Service), the Ministry of Defence and the Civil Service Commission all employ occupational psychologists. Contacting them may put you in contact with leading occupational psychologists. Universities offering the accredited Master's in Occupational Psychology will place their students on work experience, so talking to a tutor on one of these courses could also help.
Psychological Wellbeing Practitioner	This is a role that was originally developed for the NHS Improving Access to Psychological Therapies (IAPT) in England to assist with the provision of psychological therapies due to the high demand of psychological support needed for the general public. Keep an eye on www.jobs.nhs.uk for any positions available.
Sports and exercise psychology	Professional sports teams or national governing bodies of sport. You could also find work experience that involves sports coaching by locating the coaches of successful local teams or individuals. Many sports psychologists also work as private consultants, so looking through your local directory or online is a good place to start and could lead to some form of work-shadowing with them in this capacity. They can also work alongside GPs. Universities offering the master's courses in this area will also place their students on work experience, so talking to a tutor on one of these courses could also help.

will be particularly beneficial in the long run when you are preparing for possible interviews and trying to incorporate your work experience into your UCAS personal statement.

Many students who apply for psychological courses feel that they do not have any relevant experience, and fear they will not be selected for this reason. This is not true, as the vast majority of students will not have any experience in the psychological field. Any work and volunteering experience can be valuable and an opportunity to demonstrate the key skills of a psychologist, such as listening carefully, being organised and self-management, good communication skills, resolving conflicts skilfully, critical thinking, decision making, problem solving, cultural competence and self-awareness, emotional intelligence and taking initiative. All aspects of a placement are important, because from every task you will learn something about the environment in which you are working. It is highly unlikely that there will be opportunities for online work experience for students, as clients and patients are vulnerable groups so direct contact with them requires supervision by a professional.

Work experience and your personal statement

If you manage to secure work experience that is relevant to your career goal it can really improve your personal statement. To understand this, consider the following two excerpts from these personal statements:

Example 1: 'My two weeks of work experience at Great Ormond Street Hospital for Children with the paediatric psychology service was a fantastic experience. It gave me a better understanding of how psychology can be applied in practice. It also helped me to improve my communication skills and my ability to work in a team.'

Example 2: 'My career aspiration is to work in the field of child psychology. For this reason, I spent two weeks' work experience at Great Ormond Street Hospital for Children with the paediatric psychology service. During that period, I had the chance to meet doctors and nurses and listen to what their average day in a hospital is like, as well as find out general information on how they deal with patients to make them as comfortable as possible. I was particularly aware of the need to balance analytical skills and scientific knowledge with an understanding of the patients' emotional needs. This was a fantastic experience that gave me a better understanding of how psychology can be applied in practice. I am now particularly looking forward to studying modules such as child forensic psychology and clinical psychology at university. It also helped me to improve my communication skills and my ability to work in a team.'

The second example is superior to the first example in three respects. First, the opening line of the second example shows that you have considered how your work experience relates to your future goals. Second, there is more detail about what you actually learned. Third, there is a link to modules that you might study at university, which shows that you have researched the content of the courses you will be studying.

Demonstrating to the admissions tutor that you are thinking in this way can give you an edge over other applicants. The reason for this is that admissions tutors and their academic colleagues want to retain students throughout the entirety of the course. This is important to them because they want to work in a teaching environment where they feel that the students are genuinely interested and want to flourish. Furthermore, university departments are also under pressure to retain as many students as possible for funding reasons. When they decide which students they are going to give an offer to, they are hedging their bets on who they think will stay the course – so you want to show them that you are a safe bet!

When to arrange work experience

The simple answer is: as soon as possible. If you are in the process of finishing your GCSEs, then you are in a fantastic position to start looking around at the range of work experience opportunities that might be on offer so that you can select work experience that will be appropriate for you.

If you are in your first year of A levels you are also in a good position and still have time to get the kind of work experience that interests you. Ideally, you want to research your options and start applying before the Christmas holidays of your first year of A levels, with the aim of setting up some work experience for the summer months. There are several advantages to doing your work experience in this year.

- You can avoid the danger of simply trying to find any kind of work experience to put on your personal statement.
- It will be after your exams, so you won't be distracted from your studies during that all-important revision period.
- When you write your personal statement you will be able to state where you did your work experience and what you learnt. This looks much better than a personal statement where you state where you plan to be doing work experience and what you hope to learn. Again, think back to the admissions tutor who is wondering whether to take a bet on you.

However, if you are reading this and are already in your final year of A level study, all is not lost – but you must get started on arranging some work experience as soon as possible!

What if you can't arrange any work experience before you apply?

If you are unable to get any work experience by the time you apply you can always say that you have applied for such-and-such and expect to do that later in the year. If you really can't get any work experience all is not lost: for many admissions tutors the most important things are your academic potential, your personal qualities and your enthusiasm for the subject. It would be sensible to check individual university websites on their requirements before applying though.

> 'I was hoping to get into the University of Portsmouth. I could not get any psychological experience where I was living – the only placement I could find was in a local shop. I was very nervous that universities would select students with stronger work experience. After talking to my psychology tutor, he advised me to think how my placement was relevant to psychology. For instance, I referred to my interactions with customers, how I managed conflicts or difficult situations, as well as what I learnt about myself.'
>
> Charlotte

Regardless of the nature of your work experience, the way you refer to it in your statement is crucial.

> 'Working experience is not an entry requirement but candidates can use it effectively to stand out. The most common mistake that students make in their personal statements is listing all their different placements. What I am looking to read is how they can reflect in an analytic way about their experiences, how they applied their skills during this time and what kind of skills they developed. For instance, in psychology courses, I am looking for students who have developed a strong scientific mindset, such as curiosity, humility, critical thinking, as well as those who could bring different working and cultural experiences to the course. Work experience is a waste of time if there is no reflection or element of awareness. Applicants should remember that grades are fundamental to get them into the course, not working experience.'
>
> Admissions tutor at a Russell Group university

How to arrange work experience

One of the reasons why it is important to plan your work experience as soon as possible is that you may find that it takes some time to find the work experience you want at a company or institution that is willing to take you on.

Step 1: Getting the right contacts

A good way to start your research is to make a phone call to local companies, institutions and important associations, such as the BPS. Explain that you are an A level student looking for work experience related to a particular area of psychology and ask if they can help you. Sometimes you will get a 'Yes', sometimes you will get a 'No' and sometimes you will get a 'No, but I can put you in touch with someone who can help you.' The point is not to be deterred if your first two phone calls are a 'No'. Keep going! You could also send out a speculative email. If you wish to take this route, keep the content of the email fairly brief, make sure the subject is relevant and send out the email to one recipient at a time. See the example below.

To: cambsedauthority@cambs.uk

Subject: Enquiry regarding work experience opportunities

To whom it may concern,

I am writing to enquire as to whether you have any work experience opportunities available. I am currently studying for my A levels in Sociology, Psychology and Mathematics at Cambridge College and am keen to pursue a career in Educational Psychology. Should you not be in a position to offer any work experience, the details of any contacts you may have that may be able to help would be much appreciated.

I look forward to hearing from you.

Kind regards,
Catherine Harrison

Step 2: Sending a covering letter and CV

Once you have contacted people who will be able to offer you some work experience they may ask you to send in a covering letter with a CV. It is important to ensure that the content and the layout of these documents is clean and professional looking.

Covering letter

Below is an example of a successful covering letter:

---

18 Low Road
Cambridge
CB1 8ZZ

Mrs Kirby
The Educational Psychology Team
Cambridge City Council
Cambridge
CB3 2PY

1 November 2025

> **Ref: Enquiry about work experience opportunities**
>
> Dear Mrs Kirby,
>
> I am currently in my first year of studying A levels in sociology, mathematics and psychology at Cambridge College. I am seeking work experience related to the field of educational psychology so that I can learn more about learning difficulties and challenges faced by students and the day-to-day activities of professionals working in this field. I am a quick learner and a reliable and enthusiastic worker. I am trustworthy and respectful of confidential information.
>
> I would be interested in any work experience opportunities that are available. Alternatively, if you do not have any such opportunities at present I would really appreciate the opportunity to meet you at your convenience to discuss the nature of your profession.
>
> Should you require references, please contact either my personal tutor and/or my employer. Full contact details can be found on my CV, which I enclose for your consideration.
>
> I look forward to hearing from you.
>
> Yours sincerely,
> Catherine Harrison

Curriculum vitae (CV)

Standard CVs are a maximum of two sides of A4. However, unless you are a mature student, you will probably not have enough experience and training to cover two sides of A4 without leaving a lot of white space. For this reason it is better to have a full (but not cramped) CV that takes up just one side of A4. Remember that you are not applying for a job, so you do not need to overburden the person reading the CV with unnecessary detail. You just need to give them enough information to demonstrate that you will be a competent and hard-working member of staff.

In terms of style you should avoid unusual fonts and use of art. It is important to keep it clean and simple. The following are recommended.

- **Font style:** Times Roman, Arial or Calibri.
- **Font size:** 14pt for the main header, 12pt for the sub-headers, 11pt for the text. Just use bold for the header and sub-header; use italics or underlining for any lower-level headers.
- **Font colour:** black (and only black!).

In terms of content and layout there is no one correct way to compile a CV, but here is an example of a successful one.

3| Work Experience

Catherine Harrison
Address: 18 Low Road, Cambridge, CB1 8ZZ
Telephone: 07896 435675
Email: charrison@email.com

Education
2024–26: Cambridge College
2026 – A levels to be taken: Sociology, Mathematics, Psychology

2019–24: Cambridge High School
2024 – GCSEs: English (7), Mathematics (7), Science (777), English Literature (6), History (6), Geography (6), Religious Studies (6), French (4)

Other Awards
[insert any other qualifications if you have them, e.g. grades with a musical instrument, Duke of Edinburgh's Award, martial arts belts, ballet exam passes, etc.]

Employment
2023–ongoing: After School Club Assistant, Little People Nursery
Responsibilities include collecting children from local school by foot in an organised and safe manner, organising a snack, setting up and supervising activities for children and assisting with homework.

The job requires patience, an awareness of risk assessments and Health and Safety.

[insert any other employment if relevant]

Personal Attributes

- Mature and reliable
- Follows current issues in psychology
- IT competent in MS Office
- Empathetic listener
- Quick to learn
- Stamina to work long hours

Interests
I am a keen hockey player and play for my local team. I spend my leisure time playing the piano and hill walking. I enjoy watching detective dramas.

Referees

Mrs Joy Bower
Head of Psychology
Cambridge College
Cambridge
CB2 9PF

01223 123456
jbower@cc.co.uk

Miss Felicity Williams
Nursery Manager
Little People Nursery
Cambridge
CB3 7UF

01223 789101
fwilliams@lpn.co.uk

Work experience interviews

Most of the advice and guidance provided in Chapter 7 of this book is applicable to work experience interviews. However, should you be called for an interview, here are some additional points to bear in mind.

- Conduct a little bit of research about the company or practice in question. Visit its website and read its mission statement and/or the 'About us' section.
- Remember to dress smartly for interview. It is always better to be overdressed and formal than underdressed and casual.
- Offer a firm but friendly handshake at the beginning and the end of the interview and be sure to make eye contact.
- Towards the end of the interview they may ask you if you have any questions. Try to think of at least three questions that you can ask when this happens, in case they answer one or two of your questions during the interview. For instance, you could ask about the tasks that you will have to complete, the main challenges of your position, any research or project that they have conducted recently, the team you will be involved with, the culture of the organisation, what the future goals or projects of the organisation are. A good way to show interest in the company is to try to find any (positive!) recent press releases or news items related to the company to ask them about.

4 | Degree programmes in psychology

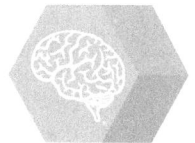

When you are choosing a degree course in psychology there are several points to bear in mind. Firstly, degree programmes will vary in their emphasis. Some will offer a general but comprehensive grounding in the subject. Others will tend to specialise in one branch of psychology.

Secondly, admission to courses is usually open to students irrespective of the A level subjects or other qualifications they have studied. However, some courses which lead to a Bachelor of Science (BSc) degree in psychology may favour students with science subjects because of the scientific or experimental nature of the degree course and the ancillary or minor subjects you may be expected to take. Degree programmes leading to a Bachelor of Arts (BA) degree may look favourably on applicants with arts A level subjects. The distinction between the two is an important one, because the titles of the awards may reflect differences not only in main course content but also in the choice of subsidiary courses you can take. Those studying for science-based courses may have option choices in neuroscience or physiology, whereas those on arts-based programmes may have options in social or developmental psychology.

This chapter will look at the different degree courses available, so as to help you identify the type of course that is best for you.

What qualities should a psychology applicant have?

'The students we look for are intelligent, open-minded, somewhat numerate and aware that while studying psychology will provide them with strong critical thinking skills and knowledge of the complexities of the human mind and behaviour, it will not solve their personal problems.'

Dr B, Senior university teacher and Fellow of the British Psychological Society

> 'We are looking for applicants with intellectual curiosity and a natural affinity to science. This is often, but not exclusively, reflected in A level choices, and we favour applications from applicants who have studied biology, chemistry, mathematics or physics, though having studied these subjects is not mandatory.'
> Dr Marc, Admissions tutor
>
> 'Our psychology applicants should show curiosity about human behaviour, strong analytical and research skills and enthusiasm for scientific study. Tutors value critical thinking, open-mindedness and clear communication. Evidence of empathy, self-awareness and motivation through academic work or relevant experience demonstrates readiness for our rigorous, research-led psychology programme.'
> K.I., Head of Admissions in a Russell Group university

BA or BSc?

At one time a psychology degree course might be either BSc or BA, but now the overwhelming majority are BSc. There are only a few undergraduate programmes that are offered as a BA, or as either BSc or BA, depending on final year options. A BSc in psychology emphasises the scientific side of the qualification being experiment- and laboratory-based, whereas a BA would often be studied alongside a social science subject such as criminology or sociology. In the past, a BSc tended to be advantageous in gaining employment over a BA. However, psychology lecturers at universities emphasise the importance of gaining a degree that is accredited. To ensure your degree is accredited, the 'find an accredited course' search tool on the British Psychological Society website filters accredited courses from non-accredited courses.

General or specialised?

Not all first degree programmes in psychology have the same aims. Some are intended to be general in nature, giving a broad and comprehensive overview of all aspects of psychology. Others, in contrast, will attempt to give a special emphasis to one aspect of the subject. You will see from the course details on university websites or in their prospectuses whether a course has a general or specific emphasis. Examples of specialised courses include applied psychology, experimental psychology, occupational psychology and social psychology. There can be some benefits in completing this kind of degree, particularly if you already know that this aspect of psychology interests you. It may also enable you to gain recognition by the relevant professional group or division of the BPS on graduation.

Single subject, joint or modular?

Most university psychology departments will offer a single honours degree in the subject, which means that your principal subject is psychology but that you may have to study other minor subjects in addition, which carry less weight in terms of marks and assessment. In addition, there are numerous examples of joint honours degrees, in which you study psychology and one other subject to the same level. Examples include psychology and management, psychology and mathematics, psychology and sociology. This kind of programme enables you to study two subjects in depth, but you may need to check whether the overall workload is slightly higher than studying for a single honours degree.

By contrast, modular degrees offer a range of different subject modules, often linked by a unifying theme. Often called 'combined degrees', they are typically provided by institutes and colleges of higher education and enable students to study psychology alongside other subjects in the social sciences or humanities. With joint degrees, and combined degrees in particular, it is important for applicants to check to see if the degree course is recognised by the BPS and gives the GBC. Without this, it will be difficult to qualify professionally. As mentioned, the BPS's website provides an online search for accredited degree courses.

Full time or sandwich?

Most degree courses in psychology are full time and last for three years, but some last four years, particularly those in Scotland, where it takes four years to gain an honours degree. A small number of programmes, called sandwich courses, give students the chance to spend their third year on practical placements in companies or with different psychological services or agencies. Students then return to their university for their final year of study.

Although sandwich courses last four years, they can provide students with a valuable opportunity to gain a year's worth of first-hand experience, which helps them not only to develop new skills but also to make decisions about which career path to take when they graduate.

Students can take advantage of work placements overseas and in the UK. Before searching for a placement, you should think carefully about the type of job you would like after graduation to ensure the placement is worthwhile and complementary to your career advancement. Usually the university has a list of institutions and companies that it has an established relationship with. However, a lot of students secure placements through networking or by making speculative applications. Placement opportunities are advertised in a number of places. It is worth checking social media channels for opportunities or contacting companies or organisations directly that interest or inspire you and submit a tailored application and CV. Most often, sandwich course students will make their own applications for placements but are supported through the process by a specialist team, who continue their support throughout the placement itself. The placement is assessed and forms part of the degree qualification.

> *'In my third year studying Psychology at Cardiff University, I had the honour of a professional placement at Headway Cardiff and South East Wales. This organisation aims to improve the life of people who have suffered a brain injury. I was involved in assessment and treatment. Due to my amazing mentor, I learnt how to carry out initial assessments as well as therapy groups. Patients could come on the day with any kind of problem, such as verbal or mobility issues, or because they were stressed and anxious, and we would try our best to make them feel better and overcome their difficulties. Not only was it a rewarding experience, but I feel that I have enhanced my clinical skills and improved my employability prospects. My mentor even asked me to work with the team after my graduation!'*
>
> Emma

A year abroad?

In one or two instances, courses have a 'year abroad' option and arrange for UK students to spend a year studying at a university outside the UK, in Europe or North America for example. A year abroad will help develop skills and broaden experience, as well as giving in-depth experience of another culture and educational system, building contacts and enhancing employability. Many of those who opt to study abroad say it is the best year of their lives. As for sandwich courses, universities provide teams to help students select and apply for their year abroad options. It is not always necessary to speak another language.

Degree course content

It is important to realise that a psychology degree will have a big emphasis on statistics and research methods. This is essential for those who want to progress to professional psychology, but it also provides invaluable training for other careers. While A level psychology can be helpful preparation for a degree course, experience of practical work and an appreciation of statistics gained from any previous qualifications (such as BTEC level 3 Applied Science) will be an advantage, as will be the ability to work independently. In 'BPS Practice Guidelines (2017, 3rd Edition)', there is a great emphasis on the importance of research for the practice of psychology. Primary and secondary research can contribute to a better understanding of how psychological processes work. Also, research assists in developing and testing the effectiveness of evidence-based interventions. These studies guide policy-makers to make informed decisions about public health.

Most degree courses offer a broad-based introduction to the subject to allow for the fact that many students will not have studied psychology before. Increasing specialisation and advanced study will follow as the programme progresses. Undergraduate degree courses accredited by the British Psychological Society provide a basic curriculum in order to meet the requirements of the Society, so when comparing courses and universities you should see some similarities in the structure and content. It is important to note that some course programmes may see a change in the coming years so always ensure you check the current edition of any prospectuses and the university websites for any changes. Below is a generalised outline on how courses are structured across universities. For further reference, there is an overview of the course structure for the University of Liverpool's BSc Psychology programme for 2026 entry on the following pages.

First year

In the first year you will be offered introductory courses in different aspects of psychology, such as development, individual differences and social psychology. You will also study a key aspect of current psychology, which is biological perspectives to explain human behaviour along with the connection between the brain and mental processes. You will also learn the basis of research methods and how to analyse data using statistical software programs. The results of your first-year assessment may well count towards your final degree result.

Second year

Courses in the second year will build on and extend subjects studied in the first year. You will study specific areas, such as clinical and forensic psychology, cognition and cognitive neuroscience, lifespan development and health and wellbeing. You may also have to complete a series of laboratory or experimental classes to give you a practical insight into psychological research methods. You will learn how to analyse data using advanced statistical methods such as ANOVA tests, and you will be introduced to psychometrics. The results of your second-year assessment may well count towards your final degree result. Some universities offer a research project in the second year.

Third/final year

In the final year of a degree programme, students usually have the opportunity to choose modules or options that interest them, options that typically reflect the research interests of the staff in the psychology department. At the same time, students will invariably undertake a major dissertation, based on a research project of their own choosing. This is a significant piece of work and the choice of topic may well have some direct relevance to a student's future career choice.

A typical course programme might consist of:

- **Year 1**: biological psychology; brain and cognition; developmental psychology; research methods and statistics 1 and 2; social psychology and individual differences;
- **Year 2**: clinical and forensic psychology; cognition and cognitive neuroscience; lifespan development, health and wellbeing; psychobiology and motivation; research methods and statistics 3 and 4;
- **Year 3**: research project; three option topics.

University of Liverpool - Psychology BSc (Hons)

Programme length: three years

The psychology degree programme at the University of Liverpool draws upon research excellence and a clear focus on transferable skills to suit a wide range of career choices. Throughout the course, students complete a number of authentic assessments to demonstrate their knowledge and skills and which allow them to practise tasks closely aligned to future employment and study demands. The curriculum is delivered in a range of formats and supported by online resources through the University's virtual interactive teaching environment (CANVAS). The degree is accredited by the British Psychological Society and provides Graduate Basis for Chartered Membership.

Year 1

Students take six compulsory modules that provide an introduction to the principal topic areas and basic methods of research in psychology. Some of the psychology modules on offer are: Biological Psychology, Brain and Cognition, Developmental Psychology, Social Psychology and Individual Differences, Research Methods and Statistics Part 1 and Part 2. In addition to lectures, the programme offers class-based practical sessions, seminars and other types of small group work. Students also have regular meetings with their academic adviser, covering general skills along with academic topics linked to the curriculum and postgraduate careers.

Year 2

In Year 1, students undertake four modules that revisit in greater depth core areas in psychology (i.e. Biopsychology and Motivation, Clinical and Forensic Psychology, Cognition and Cognitive Neuroscience, Lifespan Development, Health and Wellbeing). There are also two, more advanced modules in Research Methods and Statistics. Students continue their regular meetings with their academic advisers and also complete a small group research project, which helps develop their research and transferable skills further. As a component, these modules include a small group project under the supervision of the academic adviser. Year 1 and 2 modules are compulsory to ensure the students achieve the basic curriculum necessary for accreditation by the British Psychological Society. During Year 2, students also have the opportunity to apply for 'internships' within some of the faculty's research laboratories.

Year 3

In Year 3, students select six optional modules from four thematic pathways relating to the main areas of psychology. Although students are required to choose at least one module from each pathway, the large number of available modules provides them with the opportunity to focus their learning on topics of personal interest. Students are also given the opportunity to select the placement module, which includes a summer work placement to an organisation. In addition and central to Year 3 is the Research Project module that is undertaken by all students. This is a piece of empirical work designed as a platform for students to display the application of their prior learning to a research topic that can be related to their chosen specialisation.

Source: https://www.liverpool.ac.uk/courses/psychology-bsc-hons. Course content is subject to change; please consult the university's website or contact their admissions department for the latest information.

Degree courses in Ireland

There are 37 undergraduate degrees and diploma courses and 17 postgraduate degree courses at Irish universities accredited by the Psychological Society of Ireland (PSI). These include BA, BSc and Higher Diploma courses, as well as MA, MSc and Doctorate programmes. The pathways for further training to become a professional psychologist registered by the PSI are much the same as in the UK.

Dean, psychology graduate, 2025

How broad is the course: what areas of psychology does it cover?

The course mainly covers different areas of modern psychology relevant to the mind and behaviour, e.g. social and developmental psychology, cognition, biopsychology, atypical development and mental health disorders, and modern topics such as computer applications in psychological research, neuropsychology and science communication and public engagement.

How much choice was there in terms of unit options?

Although there were some compulsory modules I had to take, I really liked that the university offered optional modules across all four years. In first and third year, the choices were a bit more limited, but in second and fourth year, there were loads of great options. I got to study things like marketing, human resources, science communication and public engagement, organisational psychology, applied psychology and work and the psychology of self-control – all of which linked really well to my postgraduate studies in psychology and business.

Is it mainly lecture-based or do you have a lot of independent study to do?

In the beginning, the course is lecture-heavy, but as the course progresses, there is more of an emphasis on independent study. That said, despite many lectures, we were expected to carry out wider reading and research. However, our small class sizes meant that every lecture was more like a seminar with much student participation and lecture feedback.

How much practical work do you do?

The course was mainly academic and lecture-based although we did do practical lab work. We also have seminars where we analyse specific aspects of the lectures.

How are you assessed?

There is a variety of assessments. We had to write essays, complete quizzes and submit lab reports. You also have to complete an independent research project.

Is there much overlap with A level psychology?

I did my A levels in London before my family moved to Ireland, and I found there was quite a bit of overlap, especially in areas like social and developmental psychology. We also had lectures on mental health disorders, so having already studied things like phobias, depression,

OCD and schizophrenia at A level really helped me understand the material better. Research methods was another big area of overlap – I was able to build on what I'd already learned during my A level psychology course, which made things a lot easier to grasp.

What are the hardest parts of the course?

For me, statistics, definitely!

What parts have you enjoyed?

I really enjoyed studying modules that developed both my practical and analytical skills. Critical Thinking and Collaboration and Enterprise Skills helped me approach problems creatively and work effectively with others. Psychological Measurement and Assessment deepened my understanding of how to evaluate human behaviour scientifically, while Experimental Analysis of Behaviour gave me insight into the principles behind learning and behaviour. I also really enjoyed Computer Applications in Psychology Research, as it allowed me to apply data analysis and research software to real psychological studies.

Choosing a university: making a shortlist

With 191 universities offering around 1,142 BPS-accredited psychology and psychology-related courses how do you narrow down your choice to the maximum of five allowed on the UCAS application?

Things to consider:

- the grades that you are likely to achieve: there is no point in applying to universities whose standard offers are significantly higher than the grades that you are predicted, or eventually get;
- the location of the university;
- the facilities;
- the course.

You might also find it helpful to look at the league tables compiled by the national newspapers. While all league tables should be used as a guide rather than as the definitive ranking of the university, they can be useful as a starting point if you are unsure how to start looking.

The Complete University Guide (CUG) (www.thecompleteuniversity guide.co.uk) league table allows you to look at the rankings of all UK universities, or you can narrow this down to just those offering your chosen subject. In its 2026 rankings of institutions offering psychology courses, the guide placed Oxford first, followed by St Andrews, Cambridge, Bath, York, London School of Economics and Political Science, and Cardiff. The ranking is based on a number of scores, including an entry score based on A level grades achieved by students joining the courses, student satisfaction, job prospects and research quality. The CUG website allows you to reorder the tables to reflect your own criteria, or to change the weighting of the individual categories. However, try not to be too fixated on the league tables; there are many excellent courses accredited by the BPS; try to think about other aspects that you will expect from the place where you are going to spend the next three years of your life.

British Psychological Society accreditation

The BPS accredits certain psychology courses, meaning that graduates of these courses are eligible to apply for graduate membership of the BPS and for the GBC, which is required for the pursuit of professional training in psychology and is often referred to as the first step towards becoming a Chartered Psychologist. Note that eligibility to apply for the GBC is subject to achieving at least a lower second-class honours degree on a BPS-accredited course.

A BPS-accredited course will equip students with the following skills:

- effective communication, both written and oral;
- analytical and evaluative understanding of complex data;
- ability to retrieve and organise information from various sources;
- knowledge of how to handle primary source material critically;
- ability to work as part of a team;
- ability to use scientific reasoning to solve problems and look at other possible strategies;
- knowledge of how to make critical judgements and evaluations to consider different perspectives of a question;
- ability to be sensitive to contextual and interpersonal factors, including social interaction and behaviour;
- ability to work independently with thorough planning, gaining project management skills (see www.bps.org.uk).

If pursuing a career in professional psychology is important to you, consider BPS accreditation when drawing up your shortlist of courses (see www.bps.org.uk/public/become-psychologist/accredited-courses).

How to decide where to apply

Academic factors

There are many factors to consider when you choose the five courses that you are going to apply for. Some of these come down to your own personal preferences. Do you want to live at or near your home? Do you want to be in a campus university or in a large city? The only way you can really investigate these issues is by visiting universities, either by attending open days or by arranging private visits. But once you have identified the type of university you want to attend, you need to ensure that you have the suitable subjects, qualifications and predicted grades that will allow them to consider you. This requires research on your part, although if you are lucky your school careers department or university application advisers will have this information at their fingertips.

The best place to start looking at entrance requirements is the course search facility on the UCAS website, where you can search for courses using the UCAS search tool: https://digital.ucas.com/search. On the UCAS homepage select 'Courses' from the search bar and then type in 'psychology'; the website will then list all psychology courses. To narrow your search, there is a 'filter' facility in the top left-hand corner where you can choose courses according to your preferences: location, type of study (e.g. full time, part time, distance learning) and type of degree, courses with vacancies, specialised subjects, entry requirements and distance from home.

Once you have selected a course, you can 'View' the university's entry profile and this in turn will give you the option of looking at the university's entry requirements. There are sections on course-specific requirements (what A level subjects and/or GCSE background they require, for example) and academic requirements (A level grades, International Baccalaureate (IB) scores, subjects that they will not accept).

Non-academic factors

You are going to spend three or four years in the university you choose for your degree, so you ought to think about some factors other than how good the psychology course is. For example:

- Where is the university? Is it in the north of England, Scotland or the south? Is it in a town or outside? Is it a campus university or scattered around the town?
- What are the extra-curricular facilities? Do you want to be able to follow your favourite sporting activities, act or play music, or take up some new interests? Are there lots of clubs and societies?
- Is there a good system of pastoral support if you need help or for careers guidance?
- How much are the fees? What about the costs of accommodation and transport?
- And last but not least, what is the accommodation itself like?

How did you choose your university? Was it to do with the psychology department there, or other things about the place or both?

'There were several reasons why I wanted to study psychology at Oxford. First of all, the University of Oxford is one of the most prestigious universities worldwide and it has always been ranked first for psychology in the UK. My psychology tutor also finished his studies there and he described his experience as one of the best in his life. I visited the university and some colleges before I applied and I was impressed by its organisation and the support I received. The members of staff and the students were so helpful. Lastly, as a rower, I was thrilled to be accepted by a university that boasts one of the best rowing university teams.'

Maria

'For me, the most important criterion of choosing my university was the location. My parents live in London and, unlike my friends who wanted to leave home, I actually wanted to stay and study in London. I knew that I wanted to find a part-time job as an assistant psychologist while studying and I thought that in London, I would have more opportunities. I also wanted to study at one of the four universities offering the doctorate in Clinical Psychology. So, I applied to UCL, King's College, University of East London and Royal Holloway.'

Ellie

'It was not an easy decision to leave home because of the creature comforts, but at the same time, I was ready to explore, discover and create my own opportunities in life. University is the perfect way to develop your independence! Don't get me wrong – I was only a short train journey away from home, so I could go back and visit my family at any point.'

Lara

'The location was the most important to me because my parents could not afford to support me financially for my studies. Edinburgh and Glasgow universities are within the Top 10 for psychology anyway, so I was happy with the options I had.'

George

'Who doesn't know Cambridge, UCL or LSE? The reputation of the university was my primary criterion. I knew I would achieve high grades, so I only applied to high-ranking universities. My tutor also advised me to apply to well-known universities because it would make finding work in the future easier.'

James

Finding out more

All universities provide details of their undergraduate courses online. Usually they will include a summary of the course, a breakdown of the course content and options year by year, the course requirements and a careers section. This may include information on career destinations of recent graduates.

When you have a shortlist of universities you might apply to it is worth visiting their psychology departments' websites and looking at the academic staff's research interests. These can usually be found under the 'Faculties and Departments' part of the main site rather than 'Courses'. Apart from getting an idea of what areas of the course different lecturers are specialised in, it might also give you a hint about what they might like to talk about, should you be invited to an interview!

You should also try to attend as many open days as possible. After all, you are going to spend three years or more at university, so you ought to make sure you will like the place. Open days should give you the chance to see the psychology department and meet some of the staff and current students as well as to see the general parts of the university (library, refectory, sports hall, bars etc.) and possible accommodation. Visit www.opendays.com to find out details and dates for different universities and to book a place.

Sometimes students get the impression that universities are hidden behind a big wall called 'UCAS'. This is definitely not the case: the staff will be only too pleased to answer questions from potential undergraduates, so do phone them if you want to find out more, whether it is about course content or entrance requirements.

5 | The UCAS application

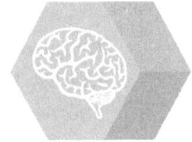

When you apply to UK universities, you do so using the UCAS system. The online UCAS application is accessed through the UCAS website (www.ucas.com), specifically through the UCAS Hub: https://accounts.ucas.com/Account/Login. You register online, either through your school or college or as a private individual. Once you have received a username and password you will be ready to log in to start your application.

Planning your application

Before we look more closely at how to complete your UCAS application it is worth mapping out a timescale for completing your application. This is important because you will need to prepare for your application well in advance. The Year 12 timeframe varies from school to school, and you are advised to speak with either the Head of Year 12 or your Director of Studies or Personal Tutor for advice. The specific dates in the following timescale are based on applications for 2027 entry. Please check the UCAS website for specific updates (www.ucas.com/undergraduate/applying-university/ucas-undergraduate-when-apply).

Year 12

- **September–March**: preliminary discussions with your teachers, family and friends – as many people as possible. Look ahead to planning open day visits and research possible work experience.
- **April–June:** discuss your university options more seriously with your personal tutor and parents. At the end of April, the UCAS search tool displays the courses available in the following year. Around a week later, the UCAS Adviser portal opens. You should also book open days and finalise work experience (see Chapter 3 on work experience).
- **June–July:** make a shortlist of universities and courses.
- **August:** work experience. Research courses in more detail, either on the university websites or by ordering prospectuses.

Year 13

- **September–January:** complete your application and send it off to UCAS – it will be accepted from 1 September onwards.
- **15 October (18:00 hrs GMT):** deadline for applying for places at Oxford or Cambridge. This is also the deadline for those who want to apply for medicine, veterinary medicine/science and dentistry courses.
- **November–December:** Oxford and Cambridge interviews.
- **13 January (18:00 hrs GMT):** deadline for submitting your application to UCAS for most undergraduate courses. If you do not get your application in on time your application will be forwarded to the universities but the admissions tutors will not be obliged to consider you. Note that all applications received after 30 June will be entered into Clearing.
- **February–April:** interviews may be held.
- **February–July:** if you have been rejected by all of your choices, you can enter one more choice using UCAS Extra between 25 February and 1 July. See page 68 for more information.
- **May–July:** you will be given a deadline from UCAS to make your final decision around this time. See 'Key deadlines' and 'Replying to your offers' later in this chapter.
- **Summer:** sit your exams and wait for the results.
- **30 June (18:00 hrs GMT):** new applications deadline, otherwise applications are entered through Clearing.
- **2 July:** Clearing opens and vacancies are displayed in the UCAS' search tool.
- **Results day:** see Chapter 9.
- **18 October:** last date to add a Clearing choice. You can still apply for courses but you need to directly contact the universities; universities with competitive courses are less likely to accept late applications.

The UCAS application

When you have logged in you will see that the online UCAS application has the following sections.

1. **Personal details:** name/middle name as stated in official documents, date/place of birth and gender.
2. **Nationality/Ethnicity:** mention where you were born and your nationality. If you have dual nationality you can submit up to two nationalities. If you are not a British citizen, you will be asked about your status (e.g. settled/pre-settled; students visa; previous visas; immigration status; when your course starts).

3. **Address**: current home address and where you have been staying for the last 3 years prior to the start of the course.
4. **Contact details**: telephone numbers, email address and postal address. This is where you can add nominate access to someone with whom universities can discuss your application if you are unavailable; it is still your responsibility to send over the application once it is completed.
5. **Supporting information**: this is where you can mention whether you, a parent or spouse has lived and worked in the EU, EEA or Switzerland).
6. **Finance and funding**: indicate how you are planning to pay your fees. Most applicants will be in the UK, ChI (Channel Islands), IoM (Isle of Man) or EU student finance. Information on finances and funding options and the opportunity to share your UCAS details with the Student Loans Company (SLC).
7. **Diversity and inclusion**: ethnicity, religious beliefs, sexual orientations, care support information and parental education and occupational background.
8. **More about you**: indicate any additional information you would like to share in your application. For example, you should include any relevant personal circumstances such as mental health conditions, long-term illnesses or being estranged from your parents. You should also mention any caring or parenting responsibilities, refugee status, connections to the armed forces (either their own service or that of a parent/carer), and whether you have received free school meals.
9. **Education**: all secondary past examination results (even if you received a 'U' grade), examinations you will be sitting in the future, places and time of study (past and present). This is also where international students can add their English Language Test (ELT) numbers.
10. **Employment history**: any time taken away from studying to work or any part-time jobs; this section is not for voluntary work.
11. **Extra activities**: any additional courses, summer schools, Saturday university, campus days, summer academies, taster courses and booster courses and activities in preparation for higher education.
12. **The personal statement**: see Chapter 6.
13. **The reference**: this is where your tutor or someone else who knows you writes about you, your suitability for the course and, if you do not yet have your A level (or equivalent) results, your predicted grades. Each school or college will have its own guidelines for the staff who write references. Guidelines for referees can be found on the UCAS website, in the 'Advisers' section. Once your application is complete, it is then accessed by the person who will write your reference; he/she checks your application, adds the reference and grade predictions and sends them to UCAS. After

that, you can keep track of the responses from the universities via UCAS Hub (see the section on UCAS Hub later in this chapter for more details). A reference cannot be given by a family member, friend, partner or ex-partner.
14. **Course choices**: which universities you are applying to, and for which courses, when you plan to start the course and whether you are planning to live at home while studying or not.
15. **Payment and submission**: here you will see a summary of the universities and courses you are applying to.
16. **Help with the application**: includes helpful tips, guidance and advice for the completion of the different parts of the application.

We will look at how to construct your personal statement in the next chapter. In this chapter we will deal with how to complete sections 1–6 and section 8.

Note: If you are applying for universities in Ireland you will need to make individual applications for each university. Contact the universities for details. (See Chapter 4 for more information on courses in Ireland.)

Completing your UCAS application

A lot of this is self-explanatory, but students often don't fill in all the boxes.

Personal details and additional information

Make sure that you make a selection for all the questions even if the answer is a 'No' (e.g. where it asks you to state whether you have a disability, most skip selecting 'none' if they have none). Make sure you fill these two sections in as fully as possible.

Student finance

It is very important to enter the correct fee code. If you want to apply for either a student loan or grant then you need to choose '02'. If you or your parents/guardians are paying for university, then select '01'. Avoid selecting '99' (unknown). More details on fees and funding are available in Chapter 10.

Course choices

In Chapter 4, we discussed what factors you need to consider when applying for university courses. Entering the courses on your UCAS application is a straightforward process, but it is worth remembering the following points.

- Be very careful when you select the university codes and course codes. There could be a difference of one digit between a three-year BA and a four-year BSc with a year in industry – you do not want to get this wrong!
- You can apply to more than one course at the same university, except for Oxford and Cambridge.
- The order in which you add the courses to your application is not related to your order of preference. The UCAS application system will simply order them alphabetically by institution.
- Remember to use your five choices wisely. Spread your choices across a range of entry Tariffs to maximise your chance of receiving offers.
- Don't forget to tick the box related to whether or not you are deferring your application.
- Don't forget to tick the box related to whether or not you will be living at home.

Education history

This is the section where students are most likely to make an administrative error. Use the following as a checklist to avoid such errors.

- Do not enter any grades for any subjects that you are still studying at A level. You should input that the qualification will be completed in June and the result should be pending. This is important because entering that the result is pending generates a predicted grade drop-down menu on the referee's UCAS web page. Without this your referee cannot complete your application.
- If you have completed and passed an AS subject you need to enter this into your UCAS application. In this instance you should input when the qualification was completed (e.g. June of the previous academic year) and enter the result you obtained.
- You can enter the results of units if you wish, but you are not obligated to do so.
- Check that the titles of the subjects you are sitting are correct (for example, are you sitting mathematics or further mathematics?).
- Make sure you have entered all your GCSE (and/or equivalent) qualifications.
- Make sure that all dates that you sat your exams are correct.
- Make sure you have entered all the exam boards correctly. It is a good idea to gather up all your statements of results and/or certificates before you sit down to complete this task.
- Enter any other qualifications that you may have, such as Functional Skills or music qualifications; they carry UCAS points and some universities will accept them as part of your overall UCAS total.

Employment history

If you have taken time away from studying to work or if you have had a part-time job this information is to be included here. You should include only paid work, not work experience. Sometimes students do not enter that they have, for example, been employed as a part-time shop assistant because they do not believe that it is relevant to their application. However, it shows the admissions tutor that you have a variety of qualities, such as the ability to work in a team and to be reliable. Moreover, the skills and qualities that you have demonstrated through being employed should be included in your personal statement. So, declaring your employment here corroborates any remarks made about your employment in your personal statement.

The reference

Since the 2024 entry cycle, the reference system has changed and specifies three particular sections that need to be addressed:

- Section 1: requires a general statement about the school, college or centre.
- Section 2: requires any information about extenuating circumstances that may have affected the student's education and achievement.
- Section 3: requires supportive, evidence-based information specific to the student and relevant to the course applied for that the referee thinks universities and colleges should be aware of.

A final point about spelling and grammar

On a final note, it really is a UCAS sin to present an admissions tutor with an application that contains poor spelling and grammar. Often, via guidance from tutors, the personal statement can be relatively error free. However, such careful checking is then undone by the student spelling their name or their subjects in lower case, or misspelling their job title in the employment section, and so on. You must be thorough when you check for spelling and grammar, not only in your personal statement but throughout your UCAS application.

Admissions tests

At the time of going to press, the Universities of Oxford and Cambridge are the only institutions requiring candidates to sit entrance exams. For all other universities, you must meet the requirements of their offer.

Cambridge

The University of Cambridge requires a common-format written assessment to be taken by applicants for all subjects except mathematics and music. The assessment for psychological and behavioural sciences takes place pre-interview, in November, and only the following colleges will ask you to take the assessment: Gonville & Caius, Homerton, Hughes Hall, Murray Edwards, Newnham, Selwyn and Wolfson. Please see www.undergraduate.study.cam.ac.uk/apply/how/admission-tests.

The Psychological and Behavioural Sciences Admissions Assessment is a 2-hour test that consists of two sections: Section One consists of three sub-sections and candidates are required to answer two of these three sections. The Thinking Skills section is compulsory, and then applicants must select two from either mathematics, biology or reading comprehension. Each sub-section in Section One contains multiple-choice questions and 80 minutes is allowed to complete the entire section. Section Two consists of a choice of four written tasks of which candidates must complete one. The total time allowed for Section Two is 40 minutes. Candidates should be aware that calculators or dictionaries are not allowed to be used under the test conditions. The assessment test is designed to measure a candidate's suitability for the course and determine the potential to achieve on an academically demanding course.

Oxford

If you apply to study experimental psychology or psychology, philosophy and linguistics at the University of Oxford, then you may need to sit the Test of Academic Reasoning for Admissions (TARA).

The TARA is a non-subject-specific test with three modules: Critical Thinking, Problem Solving and the Writing Task. The first two modules both consist of 22 multiple-choice questions that aim to assess students' critical thinking and problem-solving skills. In the third module, students must answer one essay-style question from a choice of three (in up to 750 words). You will be given 40 minutes to complete each module and students are required to take all three modules. You will need to take the test at an authorised Pearson VUE test centre. Full details and test preparation materials can be found at: https://esat-tmua.ac.uk/about-the-tests/tara/.

> **TIP!**
>
> Please do ensure that you register your details in order to sit these tests. This can be done individually or through your school or college. The deadline is usually early to mid-September and late registrations will not be accepted.

5| The UCAS Application

I've applied! What next?

Once your UCAS application has been sent you will need to register with UCAS Hub, familiarise yourself with key deadlines, reply to your offers and ensure that you understand the purpose of UCAS Extra.

Registering for UCAS Hub

Once your UCAS application has been sent you will be able to track the progress of your application on UCAS Hub. This will require a new registration via the UCAS website.

Key deadlines

For 2027 entry, the Oxford and Cambridge deadline is 15 October 2026. If the university is interested in your application, you will typically receive an invitation for interview in November and the interviews will typically be held in December. Most students will then receive a decision after January/February.

If you have applied for all other universities by the 13 January deadline, then it is highly likely that you will receive a decision from all your choices by May. If this is the case, then you have one to five weeks to make your decision, which you do via UCAS Hub. For example, if you receive all offers by 31 March, then reply by 5 May. If you have applied by 13 January you will have received all offers by 12 May. In this case reply by 2 June. If you are not holding any offers, you could add another choice in your application on 25 February in the Extra page. Last day to add another Extra choice is 1 July. If you have applied by 30 June, you should be informed about your offers by 14 July, so reply by 21 July. Clearing opens on 2 July and all applications need to be submitted by 23 September. Last day to add a 2027 entry Clearing choice is 18 October. You will find a more detailed account of UCAS application deadlines at: https://www.ucas.com/applying/applying-to-university/dates-and-deadlines-for-uni-applications

Replying to your offers

There is a variety of different kinds of response that you can receive from universities, but they all fall into one of three categories:

1. an unconditional offer, which means that you do not need to obtain any further qualifications;
2. a conditional offer, which sets entry criteria related to the qualifications you are currently studying;
3. a rejection.

When you have received the decisions from all of your course choices, then, provided that you are holding some offers, you must decide whether to accept or decline each offer. You can accept offers from only two courses. You can choose one as your 'firm' choice and another (normally with a lower grade offer) as your 'insurance' choice. You must decline any other offers that you have received.

> **Important: check your emails!**
>
> It is very important that you check your emails regularly after your application has been sent, as this is the likely way that universities will contact you if they want to call you for an interview, invite you to an open day or make any further, more specific enquiries about your application. Some universities also have their own online application process that you will be required to complete and they will invite you to complete this process via email.

UCAS Extra

If you have either been rejected from all five of your choices or you have decided to decline all your offers (or a mixture of both), then you can reapply for courses through UCAS Extra. This option is available from 25 February to 1 July. UCAS Extra allows universities to offer places on courses beyond the initial deadline. You can apply only for courses that are eligible on UCAS Extra. A list of these courses can be found on the course search engine on the UCAS website. They are the courses with an 'x' next to their name. You can apply for only one course at a time through UCAS Extra. If you have either been rejected from all five of your choices or you have decided to decline all your offers (or a mixture of both) and you do not use UCAS Extra by 1 July, then from 2 July, you will need to go through Clearing. For more information about Clearing see Chapter 9.

Taking a gap year

A gap year can be used to gain more relevant experience, to embark on personal projects such as doing voluntary work or simply to gain maturity or life experiences. See Chapter 3 for more information on work experience. Students who take a gap year typically do so either by applying for deferred entry or by applying after they have received their results.

5| The UCAS Application

Gap year route 1: Applying for deferred entry

Deferred entry allows you to apply for university entry in the year after you complete your examinations. So, if you sit your final examinations in June 2027, you would normally apply for university courses starting in September or October of the same year. By applying for deferred entry, you apply for courses starting in September or October 2028, although you submit the application in the normal way using the deadlines set out above. To apply for deferred entry, you tick a box in the 'Choices' section next to the courses you are applying for on the online UCAS application. If you are going to apply for deferred entry, you need to give details of your plans in the personal statement (see Chapter 6). The advantages of deferring your entry are as follows.

- You can enjoy your gap year in the knowledge that you have a place at university waiting for you.
- You can embark on your gap year without having to wait until you can apply through UCAS in September – this is particularly useful if your gap-year plans involve travel or work overseas.
- You engage in more work experience or voluntary work. In Chapter 3, we discussed the importance of work experience. If you defer your university entrance for a year it will allow you more time to look for the right kind of work experience. This could be particularly important if you are not sure what kind of career you wish to pursue after your degree, as you could participate in several work-experience ventures across different industries.
- You can use the time to earn money for university, especially in light of the increasing costs in tuition fees.

Note: If you are thinking of applying for particularly competitive courses you must check with the relevant institutions whether applying for deferred entry will in any way jeopardise your application.

Gap year route 2: Applying after you receive your results

Not all students who take a gap year apply for deferred entry. Some students do not submit an application (or do apply, but are not made any offers and so need to reapply) until they have completed their A levels or equivalent and have their results; that is, at the start of the gap year. Although this is not ideal there are advantages to applying after you receive your results.

- You will have your grades and so you can apply for courses for which you have already achieved the entrance requirements.
- You have more time to think about what you want to study, and where.

What happens next?

If you have applied for deferred entry your offer will be confirmed in the same way as everyone else's on results day. If you are applying after you receive your results you should aim to complete your UCAS application as soon as possible. Ensure that your personal statement clearly explains why you are taking a gap year; try to give as much detail as possible as to what you will be doing in your gap year and what you hope to gain from the experience. Importantly, try to convey to the admissions tutors the skills and qualities that you will gain during this time that will make you a better student. As you will already have your A level results there is a reasonable chance that you will hear from the universities before Christmas. Provided that (a) you choose courses that have entry requirements that you have met, (b) the courses accept post-Year 13 students and (c) you make convincing arguments for your gap year in your personal statement, you will probably receive unconditional offers.

> **Case study**
>
> 'At the end of Year 12, we were introduced to the UCAS application system at school. I immediately got nervous because I did not know which course to study at university. I was studying psychology, graphics and business for my A levels, but I did not know which one to pick for my undergraduate studies. I also had a passion for drama and music, so I was completely uncertain which pathway to follow. Although all my friends applied to university courses, I decided to have a gap year and explore my artistic side before making a decision about continuing in academia. I decided to attend theatre and music studies courses in New York instead. I studied and lived in New York for four months and it was an incredible and valuable experience! The same year I decided to go on and apply for a design course in London through UCAS. All universities that I applied to valued my experience, and my good grades were an advantage too, so I had multiple offers. I have not regretted taking a gap year because what mattered the most was to do something that I was truly passionate about, and sometimes we need to take the time and space to explore before we discover what that is.'
>
> Angel

6 | The personal statement

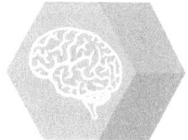

The personal statement section of the UCAS application is the only chance you get to convince admissions tutors that they should allocate one of their precious places to you, or call you for an interview. It is therefore important to take great care in writing the personal statement so that you can convince them that:

- you are serious about studying psychology;
- you have researched the course and your career options;
- you will be able to contribute to the department and the university.

How to structure the personal statement

There are many ways of constructing a personal statement and there are no rules as such, but there are recommendations that can be made. Remember that universities are academic institutions and thus you must present yourself as a strong academic bet. You have a maximum of only 4,000 characters, including spaces, to convince the admissions tutor that you are well suited to a place on their course. Each of the three sections has a minimum character count of 350 characters. Your personal statement will need to go through several drafts, with your tutor, family and friends all playing an active role in helping you to structure it.

Getting started on your personal statement can be the hardest thing to do. Do not approach this task worried about getting it perfect the first time. It is perfectly acceptable for your first draft to be a long list of things that you want to say, in no particular order! You can then use this list to start to shape your personal statement into a coherent order. When you are doing this you may want to follow the format described here.

Question 1: Why do you want to study this course or subject?

You will be encouraged to justify why you are pursuing this specific academic path; your reasons which could range from aligning with your career aspirations to a genuine passion for the subject. When contemplating your choices, you should carry out thorough research into available courses to ensure that they fit your expectations. For instance, this course could be part of an academic journey to achieve professional accreditation or simply an opportunity to explore and discover a captivating subject. Universities look for evidence that you comprehend the uniqueness among courses, even when they share similar titles, and that your chosen courses genuinely fit your needs.

The first thing that the admissions tutor wants to know is the strength of your commitment to study. Say clearly why you wish to study for your chosen degree, especially if you haven't studied psychology before. Wanting to work with people, or liking children, is not good enough. Give details of particular areas of study that interest you and say what you hope to get out of pursuing them at university level. A good way to achieve this is to start your personal statement by saying what first ignited your interest in the subject. This might have been a book or article you read, a TV programme or through contact with a family friend who worked in the field. It can also be a personal experience, such as work experience or family business. It might also have been because you chose psychology as an AS course. Again, there is no 'right' reason, but the admissions tutors will be interested in what started you on the path to your application. It is also helpful to explain how this course aligns with your career goals. Try to highlight a combination of your specific interests and academic skills. You must try to avoid clichés that could appear in any personal statement. For example, it would not be very interesting to say 'I want to study psychology at university because I am passionate about the subject.' Well, obviously . . .

Question 2: How have your qualifications and studies helped you to prepare for this course or subject?

You are expected to showcase the knowledge acquired from your A level courses. For instance, it could involve the comprehensive nature of an A level curriculum that has broadened your understanding within a field and guided your exploration towards specific areas of interest. You can refer to skills you have developed, such as research skills, critical thinking, evaluation of theories and models, effective writing of arguments – you must provide specific examples of any skills you mention. For example, 'History has helped me to understand the importance of considering the source of information and to analyse factors that can affect the interpretation of events.' Alternatively, it might encompass the acquisition of particular skills and capabilities relevant to the courses you aim to pursue further, such as advanced statistical analyses, exploration of further theories and explanations of phenomena, evaluating research evidence – again specific examples are essential. While responses will naturally differ for each student, the crucial aspect lies in demonstrating an awareness of what contributes to their potential success.

This is your chance to show that this application is not just a whim on your part, but the result of serious research. Many students think that psychology is only about the interpretation of dreams or why someone is attracted to someone else, rather than a serious and rigorous academic subject. You have to differentiate yourself from them by showing the admissions tutors that you have thought carefully about what a psychology course and/or career involves. Bookshops have sections on 'popular psychology' that contain books about psychology for non-psychologists – this is a good starting point if you wish to demonstrate an interest in the subject but haven't studied it at AS or A level. A word of warning: Don't try to impress the admissions tutors by claiming that you have read degree-level psychology books, as you may be asked about your reading if you are called for interview – stick to things that you can understand and discuss. A selection of titles is listed at the end of this book in the section on psychology texts to get you started. If you have particularly enjoyed certain parts of your AS or A level psychology course, say so and explain why. If you are new to the subject, give examples from newspapers, television, events or controversies that have appealed to the psychologist in you. It is also worth noting that some universities have been critical of the inclusion of Freud in A level specifications, so you need to be cautious if you decide to refer to Freud in your personal statement. You could also mention any lectures and seminars you have attended, as well as super-curricular activities such as academic competitions and clubs and what skills you developed through these experiences.

> 'What do I look for in a UCAS personal statement? First and foremost, a sound understanding of the subject of psychology. Students must demonstrate in their personal statements that they know what psychology is. Sounds simple, but should a student discuss dream analysis for example, this will ring alarm bells and I will call them in for an interview to find out if they are right for the course. A real winner is to demonstrate a sound knowledge of research methods and show that psychology is a scientific discipline.'
>
> *Admissions tutor*

Question 3: What else have you done to prepare outside of education, and why are these experiences useful?

At least 60% of your personal statement should deal with material directly related to your chosen course. However, it is a good idea to dedicate a paragraph to super-curricular activities, hobbies and personal interests. This could include reference to paid work, voluntary work (not specific to psychology), travel, prizes and awards such as the Duke of Edinburgh's Award, sport and music achievements, and so on. You should refer to any responsibilities you may have as a student representative, head of house, captain of a team or even leading an initiative at your college such as a charity fair.

What is important is not necessarily the activity but your reflection upon your experiences. For example, why you have chosen to highlight this particular activity, what are the lessons you extracted from it, what skills you developed through it, how these experiences advanced your thinking and the subsequent actions that you took. Importantly, you should clarify how these experiences and abilities relate to what you are planning to study and how they can contribute to your academic journey.

The following example is weak:

> 'Outside of my studies, I am head waitress at my local Chinese restaurant where I have worked at weekends for the last two years and I have also completed voluntary work at the local Food Bank. I thoroughly enjoyed both of these roles as it has allowed me to work as part of a team.'

However, a stronger version might read like this:

> 'Outside of my studies, I am head waitress at my local Chinese restaurant, where I have worked at weekends for the last two years. I enjoy interacting with the public and take pride in the responsibilities that being head waitress brings. I have also completed voluntary work at the local Food Bank, where I have sorted and categorised the wide variety of donations given (these include food, toys and books). The organiser of the Food Bank has been so delighted with my contribution and the manner in which I carry out my work that he has given me an open invitation to return at any time to assist with running the Food Bank. Both of these positions suited me as I enjoy working with older adults and members of the public. These positions demonstrate that I can be trusted with responsibility and that I am not afraid of hard work.'

Don't expect to be able to fit everything about yourself into the limited space available, and only include things that are relevant to your course or that you are prepared to expand on at interview. The idea is to whet the admissions tutors' appetite and to make them want to meet you.

A note about deferred entry

If you are deferring your university application or applying for university after you received your results you will need to explain what you will be doing with your gap year. Try to be precise and informative. For example, do not just say that you are going to find some work to fund your studies. Instead say exactly what kind of work you are going to be doing and how it will help you prepare for university. If you cannot really say much about how it will prepare you for university, then you really should research work experience or voluntary work that will enable you to do this. Saying that you are going to work 50 hours a week in a bar does not come across as good use of a year out. Even if you need to work this much to save towards your tuition fees, you should still plan to have a few weeks off during your gap year to engage in activities that will prepare you for a psychology degree.

Sample personal statements

Example 1: Izzy

Question 1: Why do you want to study this course or subject?

I first became intrigued with psychology after I was diagnosed with bipolar disorder. Throughout my years of treatment and care, I have encountered people with mental health issues from different backgrounds, and met many professional psychologists, all bringing a unique perspective to treatment. I have had the opportunity to observe and experience effective treatments, such as Dialectical Behavioural Therapy. Since psychology will always be a big part of my life, I have found that embracing my experiences and learning from them further enhanced my interest, which stems from knowledge of mental health disorders, but extends to many other aspects of psychology. In the future, I want to work as a clinical neuropsychologist, taking a leading role in assessing and rehabilitating patients with traumatic brain injuries and neurodegenerative disorders. I am excited for the opportunity to conduct research using a variety of tools, such as using scanning methods like fMRI and EEG, as well as utilising content analysis to translate behaviour from observations and interviews into quantitative categories to obtain the most thorough results. The path to this career includes the opportunity to work as a clinical psychologist first, a challenge I am looking forward to.

Question 2: How have your qualifications and studies helped you to prepare for this course or subject?

Studying biology at A level has stimulated my interest in genetics. I would like to explore the impact of genetics on mental health disorders and understand how the genetic predisposition for an illness can be triggered by environmental stressors, for example, addiction. I would like to investigate the interaction between genetic vulnerability and distressing life events. After reading about the interactionist approach in the schizophrenia module at A level, and the suggestion that brain abnormalities such as enlarged ventricles or decreased grey matter were an effect of the stress in the environment instead of the cause of schizophrenia, I researched further into the impact of stress and depression on brain structures. While reading *Neuroplasticity* by Dr Philippe Douyon, I discovered that excessively high levels of cortisol can prevent the brain from healing itself by inhibiting neurogenesis and synaptogenesis from taking place, and that this often leads to the degradation of the brain in depressed patients. This gave me a better understanding of why depression, especially in patients with brain injuries, can be so damaging.

Question 3: What else have you done to prepare outside of education, and why are these experiences useful?

I participated in an InvestIN psychology course in summer 2024, which consisted of two weeks of learning. Each day was centred around a different aspect of psychology. During the neuropsychology day, a neuropsychologist led a seminar on the brain and behaviour, followed by an interactive opportunity to conduct cognitive tests, such as word memorisation and spatial tasks. We were presented with a case study of a patient with epilepsy who was experiencing severe memory loss and were able to ask questions to deduce the reason why this was happening. This was a valuable insight into the complexities surrounding the diagnosis and treatment of patients. I found that working in a team where each person brought a unique perspective and their own method of problem solving was beneficial, and saw how valuable it was for everyone to put their ideas forward for treatment of the patient.

The complexities and intricacies of the brain are fascinating, and the aspect that intrigues me the most is neuroplasticity. To further investigate this, I signed up to be a supporter of the SameYou Charity, a charity for stroke and brain injury survivors. I was struck by the testimonies of the survivors, and how many of them had developed depression after their injury. A catalyst for this was not having access to the necessary rehabilitation or support due to a lack of healthcare resources. I feel that this is an area that can be developed further, and I would like to work in this field after my degree.

Example 2: Christie

Question 1: Why do you want to study this course or subject?

My passion for psychology and education began when I volunteered at The Human Library event. This incredible platform brought together people from all walks of life, from tattoo artists to HIV patients to the visually impaired, to share their stories and challenge prejudice. Listening to them reminded me that true education goes beyond textbooks; it is about empathy, understanding and connection. Since then, I have wanted to study Psychology with Education to become an educator who inspires others to discover their own strengths and passions. I'm particularly interested in how psychology can enhance teaching and learning, and how understanding the human mind can make education more inclusive and effective.

Question 2: How have your qualifications and studies helped you to prepare for this course or subject?

My A levels in psychology, mathematics and economics have each played an important role in preparing me for this degree. Psychology has deepened my curiosity about how people think, learn and behave, while mathematics has strengthened my analytical and logical reasoning skills essential for understanding psychological research and data. Economics has helped me explore the link between human decision making and behaviour on a larger scale, showing me how psychology applies beyond the individual to social and economic systems. Together, these subjects have given me a balanced mix of scientific understanding, problem-solving ability and curiosity about human nature, all of which I am eager to build on at university.

Question 3: What else have you done to prepare outside of education, and why are these experiences useful?

Beyond the classroom, I have actively sought experiences that connect psychology and education in real-world contexts. Over the summer, I volunteered at a language centre in Hai Phong, assisting tutors and helping design lesson plans. I enjoyed applying the concept of positive reinforcement from my psychology course to encourage students, and it was rewarding to see their confidence grow as a result. This experience also taught me the value of patience, preparation and time management in teaching.

I am also an active member of ĐÂM, a Vietnamese organisation that promotes gender equality. I have taken part in debates about gender roles and helped connect the group with charities in the UK. These experiences have sparked my interest in studying gender inequality in education and the workplace. Organising an art exhibition called *Hoa Nhan* ('Draw the Beauty') gave me further insight into gender representation and helped me develop strong organisational and communication skills, especially when over 500 people attended.

Representing my country at the Asian and Oceanian High School Students' Forum in Japan was another defining moment. Presenting on food safety in Vietnam taught me how cultural and behavioural factors shape people's choices, and it strengthened my confidence in public speaking. Reading *Grit* by Angela Duckworth also left a lasting impression on me, it showed me that perseverance often matters more than talent.

All these experiences have confirmed that I want to pursue a degree that combines psychology and education, allowing me to explore how motivation, mindset and learning intersect. I believe this interdisciplinary path will help me grow into an educator who not only teaches but also inspires positive change.

Example 3: Eliza

Question 1: Why do you want to study this course or subject?

My interest in psychology deepened after I was diagnosed with cancer and benefited from receiving psychological care during chemotherapy. Experiencing Cognitive Behavioural Therapy (CBT) first-hand showed me how powerful the mind can be in coping with physical illness. Reading *The Optimism Bias* by Tali Sharot helped me understand how optimism and pessimism can influence recovery. I was fascinated to learn that our outlook on life can even be affected by genetics because people who have shorter alleles could be genetically predisposed to being pessimistic. These experiences revealed the role of empathy in clinical settings and the importance of treating a person holistically rather than just treating their illness. I want to study psychology to understand how thoughts, emotions, and behaviour shape people's lives, and to use that understanding to help others through their challenges.

Question 2: How have your qualifications and studies helped you to prepare for this course or subject?

Studying A Level psychology has provided a strong foundation for this goal. Learning about biopsychology helped me make sense of what I observed during my work experience at a functional imaging lab, where I saw stroke patients with aphasia take part in neuropsychological tests. It was fascinating to discover that the degree of brain damage did not always match the severity of language difficulty, and that a neurologically damaged person may be able to perform tasks such as making decisions, walking and driving, yet could not form a simple sentence, which my studies helped me understand was a result of localisation of function. This experience showed me how psychology bridges theory and practice, deepening my interest in the scientific study of the mind.

Working part-time in a playgroup allowed me to work closely with children and to witness for myself the influence that role models appear to exert on their behaviour. Through observing them during playtime, I was able to see how quickly children establish roles within the classroom and how they imitated adults during play, which linked directly to my A level studies on social learning theory.

I believe I have the determination and drive to complete a psychology degree, as I have been persistently motivated to achieve my academic goals even while undergoing an intensive chemotherapy schedule.

Question 3: What else have you done to prepare outside of education, and why are these experiences useful?

Beyond the classroom, I have sought opportunities to explore psychology in real-world contexts. In the same imaging lab, I observed both the technical and human sides of research – from fMRI scans to the emotional resilience of patients adapting to communication loss.

More recently, being part of the NHS Youth Advisory Panel and volunteering with the Teenage Cancer Trust has allowed me to help improve mental health support for young people undergoing treatment. Creating a registered company to develop a peer-support app for teenagers with cancer has been one of my proudest achievements, combining empathy, leadership, and innovation with my passion for mental health advocacy.

These experiences have strengthened my determination to pursue psychology and, ultimately, a career in clinical psychology. I am drawn to understanding the complexity of the human mind – not only through research, but also through compassion and care. Psychology, for me, is more than a subject; it is a way of understanding people and helping them heal.

Applying for different courses

You write one personal statement that is read by admissions staff at the five courses for which you are applying. Each university sees only its name and course code on the application that UCAS sends to it; your other choices are not shown. If, for example, you are applying to read psychology at one university, English at another, history at a third and so on, then you cannot possibly write a personal statement that will satisfy the criteria for each of the courses. Of course, if you are applying for courses with an overlap, such as psychology and neuroscience, you can write about the areas where this overlap occurs between the disciplines, but this needs to be executed with care otherwise the admissions tutor will be puzzled as to what exactly you want to study.

General tips

- Do not attempt to copy passages from other sources. UCAS checks personal statements with anti-plagiarism software: if you have used material from someone else you will be caught out and your application will be cancelled.
- Don't be tempted to get someone else to write your personal statement. It has to sound like you, which is why it is called a personal statement.
- If you use an artificial intelligence (AI) programme, such as ChatGPT, as an assistant tool for your personal statement, be sure to use it effectively and cautiously. For example, you can use it to brainstorm ideas about how your skills and experiences can be related to the course or to check on the structure and grammar of your statement and its readability. However, do not copy,

paste and submit all or a large part of your personal statement from an AI tool and present it as your own words as universities and colleges consider it as cheating. AI tools generate generic content, and the whole point of your personal statement is to make it personal!
- Instead of explaining theories and research studies, comment on how they inspire you. Admissions tutors would like to get to know you, who you are and what you can offer in the course.
- Do research on the skills required for your course. Then analyse your experiences and make sure you relate them to these skills. Similarly, when you refer to your hobbies, explain how they have contributed to your personal development and, in turn, to the successful completion of your course.
- Although you can apply for up to five institutions or courses, you write only one personal statement, and so it needs to be relevant to all of the courses you are applying for. You will not be able to write a convincing statement if you are applying to a variety of different courses.
- Save a copy of your personal statement so that you can remind yourself of all the wonderful things you said, should you be called for interview!
- If you are planning to do so, state your reasons for applying for deferred entry and outline what you intend to do during your gap year. For example, you might be planning to find some relevant work experience in a hospital, and then spend some time overseas to brush up your language skills.

Most important of all, prior to submitting your personal statement, read through it carefully, checking for spelling and grammatical errors or parts that could be changed to make for better reading. Do ensure that you save the document. This sounds obvious but the number of students who make a fabulous start only to have to begin again because they didn't save the document will surprise you. Print off a copy and ensure your teacher or Head of Sixth Form checks it for you. Do avoid 'cheesy' lines and clichés, such as 'I have dreamt of being a psychologist since childhood', as these show a lack of imagination and seriousness. Your statement must stand out as the admissions tutor reads hundreds and your statement is your opportunity to say 'I'm here, choose me, I will be an asset to the course and this is why . . .' Grab the attention of the reader, spark interest and show intelligence and commitment in your statement.

Applying for joint honours courses

If you apply for a joint honours course, such as psychology and sociology, your application will be seen by admissions tutors from both departments, each of whom will want to see that you are a serious candidate for their course. By way of some general advice, note the following.

- Always apply what you have studied/read/done to your course.
- Balance the argument for studying both courses.
- Try to link them – can you see why these two are joint honours?
- Make sure you know why you want to study joint honours and not a single honours degree.

Many universities offer very detailed advice about what they are looking for in a personal statement, and some will reject you if your statement does not conform to what they are looking for. Even if you are not going to apply there, the London School of Economics and Political Science website contains some very useful advice on writing personal statements. Visit: www.lse.ac.uk/study-at-lse/Undergraduate/Prospective-Students/How-to-Apply/Completing-the-UCAS-form/Personal-Statement.

7 | Succeeding in your interview

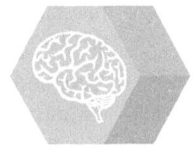

Universities interview prospective undergraduates because they want to make sure they are admitting people who will last out a three- or four-year course, making the most of life at university and achieving a good degree. Admissions tutors do not want to rely purely on the UCAS form because, let's face it, most students will have had lots of help with the personal statement and your referee will probably say only nice things about you! At interviews university staff can see what you are really like as a person, how enthusiastic you are about studying psychology and how good you are at thinking about questions you have not had a chance to prepare for. Interviews can take place in person or online.

You may not get called for interview at all. However, a number of universities – Oxford and Cambridge, and usually those with the highest ratio of applicants per place – still ask students to attend a formal interview, and others combine open days with more informal meetings. Some universities invite students for interview only if the course or admissions tutor has questions about the personal statement that they want to discuss with the candidate (see Chapter 6).

If you do apply to a university that interviews applicants, don't worry: the interview is a chance for you to demonstrate to the selectors your suitability for the course. It will not be an unpleasant experience, as long as you do your preparation.

Preparation for interviews

Essential preparation includes rereading the personal statement from your UCAS application. This may well form the basis of preliminary questions (which are meant to put you at your ease) – and if it proves to be a mass of fabrications, the interview is doomed from the start!

Prepare to demonstrate your enthusiasm for the subject and your insight into it by reading about the latest research, focusing on what makes a particular study interesting and newsworthy: are the findings unexpected or controversial? What are the practical implications? Were there ethical issues in carrying out such research? Newspapers and news websites will regularly report new research in psychology, so they are an excellent starting point. You can also check the BPS

Research Digest via the website (www.bps.org.uk), which summarises recent studies.

Familiarise yourself with the course you are applying for: Make sure you understand what the compulsory elements and optional units are. You may already have ideas about which options you would like to take.

It is important to reflect on yourself. Consider in advance what your strengths and weaknesses are, or how you could contribute to the course. Do not hesitate to reveal a weakness, but try to turn it into a positive. Admissions tutors prefer candidates who can demonstrate that they have the coping mechanisms to deal with stressful and difficult situations; they are looking for candidates who are not going to give up if they face a problem during their university years.

It is also important to reflect on your experiences. If you have done any relevant work experience, make a bullet-point list of what you did, what you saw, whom you met and what you learnt from the experience. If possible, link this to the course content or your future career goals.

On the day, be punctual, make sure you wear something clean and smart but comfortable. You don't have to dress formally but you should appear to be taking your application seriously. Basically, you need to show some respect for the admissions tutors in your appearance and not look as if you just got back from a festival. After all, it's an important day for them as well as you.

Do not 'over-prepare'; admissions tutors are interested in seeing the real you, not an airbrushed, carefully rehearsed version of you.

If the interview is online, ensure that you are in a place where you feel comfortable, is quiet and free from distractions. Also, make sure that your internet connection is stable.

Finally, take your time to answer the questions – think first.

General hints for interviews

While the number of people conducting the interview and the length of time it takes can vary, all interviews are designed to enable those asking the questions to find out as much about the candidate as they can. It is important, therefore, to engage actively with the process (good eye contact and confident body language help) and treat it as a chance to put yourself across rather than as an obstacle course trying to catch you out. Don't worry, almost everyone gets anxious about interviews and your interviewers will make allowances for this. In fact, if you are too relaxed they may conclude that you are not that bothered about a place.

Interviewers are more interested in what you know than in what you don't know. If you are asked something you can't answer, say so. To waffle (or worse, to lie) simply wastes time and lets you down. The interviewers will be considering the quality of thought that goes into your answers; they will not expect you to know everything already. Demonstrate the qualities admissions tutors are looking for in students: critical thinking, decision making, problem solving, creativity, logical thinking, formulating arguments, and coherent, concise and precise verbal skills. Demonstrate the A level skills you have acquired such as description, application and evaluation. Use strengths, limitations and criticisms of theories and models to demonstrate your critical thinking. Additionally, do not forget that psychology is a science and they might ask you to demonstrate how psychology is in line with the features of science.

Some tutors may challenge your way of thinking by asking you to look at a problem from a different perspective. What they are looking for is whether you can engage with new concepts and how flexible your way of thinking is. Tutors are not there to trick you, ignore you or catch you off guard, but to stretch your skills to assess your academic potential.

> **TIP!**
>
> Pauses while you think are perfectly acceptable; don't be afraid to take your time.

It is possible that one, or more, of the interviewers will be your tutor(s) during your time at university. Enthusiasm for, a strong commitment to and a willingness to learn your chosen subject are all extremely important attitudes to convey. The people you meet at interview not only have to judge your academic calibre, but also have to decide whether they would enjoy teaching you for the next three to four years. Try to demonstrate your enthusiasm by mentioning books or articles that you have read, or topics that you enjoyed as part of your AS or A level psychology course.

> *'In a psychology course, it is important students have a good understanding of what the discipline of psychology entails, what methods researchers use to study the different phenomena and their rationale, what procedures they follow to conduct their research and what features make a study scientific. I am looking to see motivation and enthusiasm for psychology, as well as the potential to develop the academic, research and clinical skills that they need as professional psychologists. Candidates try to portray themselves as perfect humans, which is not sensible.'*
>
> Dr A, Senior Tutor

> 'In an interview, we're looking for applicants who show genuine curiosity about psychology and a clear understanding of what studying it involves. We're not expecting them to know everything, but we want to see that they can think critically, question ideas and connect theory to real-life examples. It is important that they can reflect on their experiences, whether academic, personal or extracurricular, and explain what they learned from them. We also look for good communication skills, self-awareness and the ability to discuss ethical or social implications thoughtfully. Above all, we want to see enthusiasm, motivation and an open-minded approach to learning.'
>
> K.I., Head of Admissions in a Russell Group university

An ability to think on your feet is vital. Over-rehearsed responses never work: they appear glib and superficial and, no matter how apparently spontaneously they are delivered, they are always detectable. Putting forward an answer step by step, using examples and factual knowledge to reinforce your points, is far more professional, even if you are not completely sure of what you are thinking and saying. Use short sentences to keep track of what you are saying. That said, it is also sensible to admit defeat: knowing you are beaten is a more intelligent thing than mindlessly clinging to the wreckage of a specious case.

It is possible to steer the interview yourself, to some extent. If, for example, you are asked to comment on something you know little about, confidently replacing the question with another related one shows enthusiasm. Don't waste time in silences that are as embarrassing for the panel as for the candidate.

Questions may well be asked about your extra-curricular activities. Again, this is to put you at your ease: your answers should be thorough and enthusiastic, but not too long! Some more specific psychology-related questions are listed on the following pages.

HOPE

Use the acronym HOPE to remind yourself of the personal qualities that you should try to display at the interview:

Honesty;
Open-mindedness;
Preparedness;
Enthusiasm.

Specimen interview questions

The first thing to remember is that it is impossible to prepare for all the questions that might be asked in an interview. The interviewers will deliberately want to ask questions that make you think on your feet. So you might as well stop worrying about it beforehand! There are a few predictable questions you should be able to answer, however, without a long pause for thought. The list below includes some of the more obvious questions you might be asked as well as a few calculated to get you thinking and talking on the spot.

1. Why have you chosen to study psychology?
2. Why did you choose this university to study psychology?
3. What first interested you in psychology?
4. What do you understand by the word 'psychology'?
5. What do psychologists do?
6. What would you like to do after graduating?
7. Is psychology a science?
8. What are the differences between psychology, psychiatry and psychotherapy?
9. What have you done to investigate psychology?
10. Why did you/didn't you choose to study psychology at A level?
11. Have you read any books on psychology?
12. What particular areas of psychology interest you?
13. How do you keep up with current issues in psychology?
14. Tell me about something that is related to psychology that has been in the newspapers recently.
15. New theories in psychology need to be tested: how do psychologists go about testing theories?
16. Give me an example of an experiment that tests a psychological theory.
17. Is it ethical to experiment on human subjects?
18. Describe some of the links between biology and psychology.
19. Why is a knowledge of mathematics important when studying psychology?
20. Who should judge whether someone has a psychological disorder?
21. How do you cope with stress?
22. How do you relax?
23. What are your best/worst qualities?
24. I see from your personal statement that you are interested in (insert topic/interest). Tell me about it.
25. What are you going to do in your gap year?
26. Why are you taking a gap year?
27. What do you like about our psychology course?
28. What options will you choose in the second year?
29. Why did you choose a joint honours degree?

30. Do you know why some psychology degrees are awarded a BA and some a BSc?
31. Are psychologists allowed to divulge information given to them in confidence by a patient?
32. Do you think psychometric testing is a valid way of deciding whom to appoint for a particular job?
33. What is synaesthesia?
34. Why do people dream?
35. Is intelligence genetic or learnt?
36. Tell us about yourself. What are your main strengths and weaknesses?
37. Tell us about a difficult situation you have faced, and how you resolved it.
38. What did you learn from your work experience?
39. Tell us about a theory you have learnt; how would you evaluate it?
40. Tell us about a research study you have read; how would you evaluate it?
41. Are the brain and the mind the same thing?
42. Do robots have consciousness?
43. What is crime? How do we determine what is considered a crime?
44. What is normal for humans? How do we decide if a behaviour is abnormal?
45. Does Google know us better than we do?
46. What is meant by diversity? Is it limited to ethnicity, race and culture? What is neurodiversity? Why is diversity important?

In addition to these questions, look out for current debates in psychology that may have been in the news. These could very well provide topics for interview questions. Look out for news of research that has social and ethical implications. For example:

- A 2024 report by the Centers for Disease Control and Prevention highlighted improvements in some youth mental-health metrics but also rising school-based violence. How would you interpret this mixed result – improvements in mental health but increases in school-violence and absenteeism? What might this suggest about how we measure adolescent wellbeing?
- A 2024 study found that perceived stress mediates the relationship between social support (from family/significant others) and mental health outcomes. If you were designing an intervention based on this study, how would you apply the finding that family support reduces stress and thereby helps mental health?
- Research in 2025 indicated rapid expansion of digital mental health tools (apps, VR, generative AI) but with concerns about evidence base and equity. What ethical and methodological issues arise when deploying digital mental health tools, especially for underserved communities?

- A 2024 pilot clinical trial at Stanford Medicine found that a ketogenic diet gave improvements for severe mental illness. What are the implications of dietary interventions being integrated into mental health treatment? How would you assess the merits and risks?
- A 2024 WHO media release flagged screen use and mental health among adolescents. Given this concern about screens and youth mental health, what kind of research design would you propose to clarify cause vs effect?
- A 2025 study showed that exposure to negative online content can worsen mood and may initiate a cycle of harm. What strategies could psychologists use to help individuals break a cycle of negative digital content and mood deterioration?
- New research from 2025 outlined a belonging-intervention that improved mental health and academic outcomes for BIPOC/first-generation students. How important is the role of psychological interventions designed for specific groups (e.g. first-gen, BIPOC), and what challenges might arise in their implementation?
- A 2025 paper described psychologists' use of social media for social-justice advocacy and highlighted ethical issues. Should psychologists engage publicly on social media about mental health issues and social justice? What boundaries or guidelines should apply?
- A 2024 study found that, even post-COVID, anxiety and depression rates remain significantly higher than pre-pandemic. What are the long-term implications of elevated mental health issues following a societal crisis like a pandemic? How might psychology respond?
- A 2025 news item reported that one in four young people in England have a common mental health condition, with rising self-harm and suicidal ideation. What does this statistic imply about the demand for psychological services and the role of early intervention?
- A 2024–25 review noted that the most popular psychology/neuroscience studies included those on childhood trauma, brain mechanisms, digital health tools. Why do you think studies about childhood trauma and brain mechanisms generate such high interest, and what are the responsibilities of psychologists when interpreting these findings?
- A recent digital-future issue by the British Psychological Society focused on online therapies, social media, fitness apps and the impact of large language models. How might large language models or AI-driven tools change the way psychological therapy is delivered? What are possible benefits and drawbacks?
- A 2024 study related childhood trauma to increased substance use and physiological effects (heart rate, blood pressure) in adolescents. Considering the link between trauma, behaviour and physiology, how would you approach treatment for an adolescent presenting with both mental health and substance-use issues?

- A 2024 Centers for Disease Control and Prevention data set showed racial/ethnic disparities in mental health issues and access to care. How important is cultural competence in psychology, and what steps would you take to ensure inclusive care and research for minority groups?

These are the sorts of debates that academic and professional psychologists are involved in, so you might as well start getting used to them now! Please see Chapter 11 for a list of useful online psychology resources.

> 'Most of the students include a series of books and articles they have read. They explain thoroughly about the content, but what I am looking for is a critical mind; how what they read was relevant to them, how it influenced their way of thinking and whether they provided any criticisms to it. I have read most of the books and articles that candidates mention, but they need to remember that I don't want to know just their choices; I would like to get to know them through their choices.'
>
> Dr M, admissions tutor

Asking questions of your own

At the end of the interview you are normally given a chance to ask questions of your own. If you have none, say that the interview has covered all the queries you had. It is sensible, though, to have one or two questions of a serious kind – about the course, the tuition and so on – up your sleeve. Don't ask anything that you could, and should, have found answers to in the prospectus. It is also fine, even desirable, to base a question on the interview itself. This marks you out as someone who listens carefully, pays attention, is curious and who is keen to learn.

Above all, make the interview panel remember you for the right reasons when they go through a list of 20 or more applicants at the end of the day.

The interview itself: general reminders

- Reread your personal statement to anticipate the questions you may be asked.
- Make sure you arrive early.
- Dress comfortably, but show that you are taking the interview seriously: wear smart, clean clothes.
- Make eye contact.

- Be willing to listen as well as talk, and don't be afraid to ask questions if you are unsure of what the interviewer wants.
- Be willing to consider new ideas.
- Be yourself.
- Above all, be enthusiastic!

> **Case studies**
>
> 'I had an interview with the University of Exeter. They sent me a case study to prepare before the interview along with some instructions. It was mentioned that during the interview, I was expected to show critical thinking of clinical applications based on this case and also knowledge of the NHS Talking Therapies for Anxiety and Depression services. I did some quick online research about these services and created some key points to keep in mind for the interview. I also had a session with my psychology tutor to get some additional advice on how to approach the interview. We practised some tricky questions together, so I felt more confident. Preparation is key but do not overdo it. Responses need to be natural and not pre-rehearsed. It helped me a lot to have some "mental lists", bullet points to use for specific questions. It is essential that you reflect on yourself, your skills and experience before the interview and to have thought about something as simple as your strengths or weaknesses. I would also advise students to refresh their knowledge, key theories and figures and some research studies to use as evidence in their answers. And be yourself.'
>
> Sarah
>
> 'I had an interview for psychology at Cambridge. I was slightly nervous because I knew how competitive it would be. I made sure that I was in Cambridge the night before and stayed in a hotel. This allowed me to get a good night's sleep and a nice hotel meal and removed any worry about train delays. The interview was short; they asked me to design a study regarding the effectiveness of a memory mobile application, to analyse graphical displays regarding gender differences in emotional expression and to describe implications in society if everyone was able to scan their brain and detect abnormalities in their brain functioning.'
>
> Helen

8 | Non-standard applications

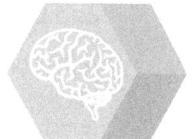

Although this book focuses mainly on traditional applications where students are doing A levels (or IBs or Scottish Highers, etc.), with an application based on them, there are those who apply to study psychology on a BPS-accredited course with a view to changing their occupation. In 2024, 13,090 UCAS applications for psychology were from those aged 21 or over.

Mature students

Mature students (in general, applicants who are over the age of 21) generally fall into three categories:

1. Those with A level (or equivalent) grades that are sufficient for entry onto a psychology degree course, but who have been working or have been involved in other activities since they completed their studies. For these students, all of the advice in the previous chapters is applicable. They would need to apply through UCAS, as previously described. The main difference might be in the 'Employment' section of the application, where more detail will be required, and in the personal statement, which should contain an overview of what the candidate has been doing since he or she sat their school exams.
2. Those who have already studied at university, but in a different subject. For these students, there are a number of options that will depend on why they are looking at a psychology degree. If the eventual aim is to qualify as a Chartered Psychologist, they should take advice from the BPS about their possible options. In some cases, it may be necessary to study psychology at degree level, but it might be possible to undertake further postgraduate training without the need to do this.
3. Those without the necessary qualifications to be accepted onto a degree course. Potential applicants in this position should contact university admissions departments to discuss their individual situation. They may be advised to take A levels (or equivalent), possibly on an accelerated one-year course offered by some sixth-form colleges and colleges of further education, or there may be Access or Foundation courses that are more appropriate.

The importance of the personal statement and CV for mature student applications

Although a certain amount of factual information will be available to the selectors through reading the UCAS application (education details, qualifications, employment details etc.), it is important that they are able to understand fully the route that the mature applicant has taken to get to the point where he or she is applying for psychology courses. As one admissions tutor says: 'What I want to see is a narrative of the events and decisions that led to the application. Why apply now? What have you been doing since you were at school? What caused the change in direction?'

Some of this can be explained in the personal statement. For example:

> 'I studied Accounting after my A levels, and thought that I would follow a career in banking to ensure a secure financial future. I started working at a bank, where I was in daily contact with customers helping them with their requests. I was enjoying my job, but something did not feel right; I felt that something was missing, that I was not achieving my full potential. At the same time, my best friend's son was in serious trouble at school and he was asked to attend a youth centre to improve his behaviour. I started volunteering there. After four years in banking, I realised that I was more interested in communicating with people than advising them on their finances. The following year, I was offered the Lead Team position at the youth centre – and that is why I pursued a career in psychology at the age of 27.'

If you cannot tell the whole story using the UCAS application and personal statement, then put together a CV and send it directly to the admissions departments. They will then attach this to your UCAS application. In order to ensure that they can match up the CV with your application, send the CV after you have been given your application number from UCAS, and quote this in all correspondence with the universities.

The CV should include details of all employment, and should fill in any gaps. For example:

> **September 2025–August 2026: Team Leader, Youth Centre, London**
> Led a team of volunteers assisting teenagers in developing skills relevant to careers orientation.
>
> **September 2023–August 2025: Volunteer, Youth Centre, London**
> Assisted a small group of teenagers in developing their communication and interview skills.

> **September 2021–August 2023: Bank Cashier, NatWest Bank, London**
> Responsible for assisting customers with financial requests.
>
> **September 2020–August 2021: Customer Information Assistant, NatWest Bank, London**
> Helped customers find relevant information for their financial requests.

Remember: universities welcome mature students, as they value their experiences and their commitment to their subject. They will be only too happy to give you advice in advance of your application.

For over 50 years, the Open University (OU) has provided a route for mature students to study for a degree part time through distance learning. This enables people to gain a degree while pursuing a career and/or raising a family. The OU psychology department has been home to many leading researchers, and it offers certificates, diplomas and degrees. There are 11 degree courses, from which seven are BPS-accredited, five are psychology diplomas and five are psychology certificates. In the past few years an increasing number of under-25s have signed up for OU courses. This might be an option worth considering, depending on your personal circumstances. The OU is not part of the UCAS system, so you will not need a personal statement or reference, but it is possible to get access to funding as with conventional universities. For more information visit www.open.ac.uk/courses/psychology.

International students

Students who are from outside the UK need to apply for psychology courses in the same way as UK students – using the online UCAS application (www.ucas.com). The UCAS website contains a section for international students which describes the process and the deadlines in detail. The 'Education' section of the UCAS application contains drop-down menus of all current and pending international qualifications, not just UK exams.

International students can often be at a disadvantage, not because they are applying from overseas but because they or their advisers are not as familiar with what the selectors at UK universities are looking for in a strong application. This affects two sections of the application:

1. the personal statement;
2. the reference.

The personal statement for international students

The UCAS personal statement needs to focus on the course itself, and what the applicant has done to investigate it. The advice given in Chapter 6 is equally applicable to international students, and should be read carefully. It is important to remember that the student is 'selling' him or herself to the admissions staff by demonstrating suitability for the course, not based on personal achievements or qualities.

In some ways, as an international student, you have certain advantages on your side. For instance, you can compare the differences between your own culture and the UK and what this might mean for psychological theories. If you have already been in the UK for some time doing your A levels, you can also demonstrate that you are used to living independently away from home.

References

References are an essential part of your application as they illustrate your academic potential, your approach to studying and your suitability for the course. Often, a promising application is rejected because the person providing the reference is unfamiliar with what is required, and the selectors have no choice other than to reject because they are not given enough information. Your referee should be a subject teacher, school adviser or the head of year. If you are no longer in formal education, an employer, volunteering supervisor or trainer can provide a professional reference. Avoid using family, friends or partners as your referees.

You can nominate the referee who you would like to support your application. Whoever you choose, inform them what you are planning to study so they provide a relevant reference. If you do not hear back from them, you can ask a different person to provide the reference. Give them enough time to provide it and you will be notified once they submit the reference.

Only one reference is submitted with your application; if you would like to submit more, you need to contact each of your university or college choices to ask if they accept additional references.

UCAS references need to focus on the following:

- the key elements of the student's academic performance to date;
- the student's suitability for the course and level of study;
- the student's skills, personal qualities, extra-curricular activities and interests that are relevant to the course;
- providing further evidence on information given elsewhere in the application.

From the 2024 entry cycle, there has been a change in the submission of references to include three specific sections (see Chapter 5). If you are unsure whether the person who will write your reference fully understands what is required, show them the section on the UCAS website called 'international advisers': www.ucas.com/advisers/help-and-training/guides-resources-and-training/international-advisers.

Language requirements for international students

Most UK universities require an International English Language Testing System (IELTS) score of at least 5.5 to study psychology (with a minimum of 5 in each of the four sub-tests). These scores may vary across universities but most universities require an IELTS score of at least 6.0 or 6.5. Other qualifications such as IGCSE (International GCSE) English or PTE Academic (Pearson's English test) are also recognised. You should check carefully what the English language requirements of your chosen universities actually are: you do not want to be in the position of gaining the A level grades to take up an offer, only to fall down on the English requirement.

If you have not completed any studies in the UK, you may need to pass a Secure English Language Test (SELT) as part of your Student Visa application. (For more information, please check www.gov.uk/student-visa/knowledge-of-english.) If you have studied in the UK already, you will be expected to demonstrate progression in your use of English for your university visa application. If you studied outside the UK a degree-level academic qualification that was taught in English, you have to apply through Ecctis (https://qls.ecctis.com/) for confirmation that you qualification is equivalent to a UK degree.

> 'Studying A levels in English while being from Hong Kong has been both challenging and rewarding. At first, adapting to a different academic style and expressing complex ideas in a second language required extra effort. However, it greatly improved my critical thinking, writing and communication skills. Learning psychology, economics and other subjects in English also helped me engage with global perspectives and research more confidently. It strengthened my independence, adaptability and ability to think across cultures, skills that are invaluable for studying psychology at university.'
>
> *Lee*

> 'Coming from a privileged background in Malaysia, my parents had the means to offer me a great education, as part of which I learnt three foreign languages. I studied law and started working as a lawyer at an international law firm. My specialisation was to help women who had experienced domestic abuse or trafficking. I soon realised that I would like to be able to support these women, not only legally but also psychologically. Although I was a mature student, UK universities welcomed my applications and I was accepted onto all four undergraduate psychological courses that I applied for.'
>
> *Aisha*

'Studying for A levels in the UK was initially intimidating. I had learned English as a second language in Russia, and the transition was challenging. I encountered many unfamiliar words at first, but I wasn't afraid to ask about their meanings in class. I frequently practised my exam skills, and my school provided additional writing classes for students who, like me, didn't have English as their first language. Patience, consistent assignment writing, regular practice with exam papers and active participation in class discussions to express opinions were all methods that contributed to improving my English.'

Denis

Visa requirements

Since 1 January 2021, all international students, including European Union (EU), European Economic Area (EEA) and Swiss nationals, who enter the UK to study need to follow the 'Student' immigration permission route. EU, EEA and Swiss nationals are allowed to visit the UK for up to six months for short-term study without a visa, but this is not for degree-level courses.

If you require a visa to be in the UK and, if your course is longer than six months, which psychology courses invariably are, then you will need to apply for a Student Visa. Before you do this, you will need a licensed student sponsor; for this, your university will request various pieces of information from you, including your education transcripts and passport. They will produce a Confirmation of Acceptance of Studies (CAS) letter for you once you have given them all the information and paid a nominated deposit. You will then need to take the CAS letter to the UK embassy in your country in order to obtain a visa for studying. Do not delay in this process, as obtaining a visa can take time, and this will vary from country to country. Also, be aware that there are time limits on how long you can study with a Student Visa. You can find more information from the UK Council for International Student Affairs (www.ukcisa.org.uk).

Students with disabilities and special educational needs

If a candidate has a health or learning difficulty or disability, there is a specific section on the UCAS application in which to declare this (i.e. Section 8: More about you). Under the personal details section, you must indicate the type of disability/additional needs you have by selecting the most appropriate from the list available. Be open and explain any sort of needs you may have. Universities would like to get to know you and ensure the availability of any support for you. There is

8| Non-standard Applications

also a section where you are able to elaborate and give further details. Most universities require that you register or make an appointment with Student Services in order for them to carry out any assessments that may be necessary. Universities value and accommodate diversity, so lots of help is available. Visit individual university websites for more information.

9 | Results day

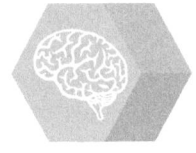

You have done all of the hard work – your personal statement, the interview, the examinations – and you are now waiting for your results, the results that will determine whether you have achieved what you need to take your university place. This chapter explains what happens when you get your results, and, if you have achieved grades that are either better or worse than expected, what other options are available to you.

When the results are available

- A levels – mid-August;
- IB – early in July;
- Scottish Highers – first week of August.

Ask your school or college for the exact date and time that they will issue you with the results. Whichever of the exam systems you are sitting, you need to act quickly if you:

- have missed the grades or scores that you require to satisfy your firm offer;
- are not holding any offers and wish to apply through UCAS Clearing.

What to do if you have no offers: UCAS Extra

If you apply for five courses and either receive no offers or decline all the offers you get, you are eligible for UCAS Extra. Extra operates from the end of February to the beginning of July and allows you to add one additional choice at a time.

To find a course using Extra, use the UCAS search tool and the filter 'Show courses with vacancies'. Next, contact the universities and colleges listed to check if they'll consider you. It's recommended that you call the university to which you want to apply before you add the Extra choice, to check whether there is space on the course and to discuss your suitability. To apply for the new course, you need to add the details to your application.

Your chosen university will consider your application, and, if this is unsuccessful, you can add another Extra choice as long as it's before

July. If you have not heard back from the university within 21 days, you can add another Extra choice (again, before July).

Once you have received an offer through Extra, you'll need to either accept or decline it. Ensure that you respond by the date displayed on your homepage, or your offer will be automatically declined.

Don't worry if you don't receive the offer you'd hoped for in UCAS Extra – you can still participate in Clearing.

What to do if things go wrong during the exams

Occasionally, students will underperform in an examination through no fault of their own. This could be through distressing family circumstances (a serious illness to a family member, for example), illness in the run-up to the exam (or during the exam) or unforeseen circumstances such as late arrival to the exam due to problems with public transport. In all cases, after the examination, you should immediately inform the universities that this has happened to you. You should, if possible, get your referee to give the details to the universities and provide documentary evidence, such as a letter from your GP.

What to do on results day

You can collect your results from your school or college, or you can arrange to receive them via email or post. It's a good idea to go into school or college to receive them in person, so that you can get support and advice from teachers and careers advisers about your options if you need it.

UCAS receives your exam results directly and will update UCAS Hub with the outcome of your university applications on results day. The system will be busy, so you might need to be patient to find out whether you've been successful.

You'll need to have the following things ready to ensure that you can do everything you might need to on results day:

- UCAS Hub login details;
- UCAS ID number;
- UCAS Clearing number, if you go into Clearing;
- details of your offers;
- the UCAS and Clearing numbers of your chosen universities;
- a working phone and computer, so you can communicate by phone or email.

When you do get your results, one of four things will happen:

1. You receive confirmation of your place from the university you selected as your firm choice, and accept it.
2. You have not met the offer from your firm choice but you will receive confirmation from the university you selected as your insurance choice and accept it.
3. You have met and exceeded the offer made by your firm choice and decide to try to swap courses by going through Clearing (see below).
4. You have not met the requirements of any offers and need to go through Clearing.

If you have achieved the grades that meet the offer made by the university you selected as either your firm choice or insurance choice and are happy with this offer, then congratulations! You do not need to do anything. However, if you want to decline your firm place and make use of UCAS Clearing or have not met any offers and need to use Clearing, then read on.

What to do if you exceeded the grades that you expected

If you have met and exceeded the conditional requirements of your firm choice and it has accepted you – therefore converting the conditional offer into an unconditional one – you could potentially swap your place for one on another course that you prefer by using the 'decline my place' button in the application. The phrase 'met and exceeded' means that if you needed BBB you would have achieved ABB or better. It doesn't necessarily mean that you just got more UCAS points. For example, if you needed BBB and achieved A*BC, then you would have accumulated more UCAS points with A*BC than you would have if you had only achieved BBB. However, you would have still failed to meet one of your grade requirements. In cases like this, your eligibility will depend on whether your offer was based on UCAS points or grades.

If you decide to pursue a different course you have to go through UCAS Clearing. Since more than 50,000 students get a course through Clearing, it is highly recommended that you find the course of your preference as soon as possible as this is a first come, first served system.

Use the Clearing search tool to find all the available courses. Once you have found an alternative course, you will need to phone the university yourself. When you call the university, you will need to give them your UCAS personal ID number and explain straight away that you have exceeded the grades of your offers and are applying through Clearing. Be prepared to answer questions about why you really want to study on that course. If they agree to accept you, and you in turn agree to accept them, this will happen during the phone call. Once you receive an offer, you can add it in your application so the college or university can officially accept you. At this stage, your status on UCAS Hub will change. Remember that if you do not find an alternative course that you want, or do not get accepted onto an alternative course, your original firm offer will still stand.

Make sure that you think carefully about the courses and universities, if you decide to go through Clearing. Just because a university has higher entry requirements or is considered to be more prestigious, it does not necessarily mean that you will enjoy the course more. Consider carefully why you selected your initial firm choice and check whether your reasons are still valid and you have the same interest and passion to study a new course.

What to do if you have no confirmed offers

If you are not holding any offers there could be several explanations.

- You may have missed the required grades of both your firm and insurance offers.
- You may have achieved the right grades but not in the right subjects.
- The university or UCAS may not have received your results. The examination boards send the results automatically to UCAS, but if you sat an exam at a different centre, for example, then this may not have happened.
- The examination system that you sat does not automatically send the results to UCAS – for instance, if you sat overseas qualifications.

In the cases of achieving the right grades but not in the right subjects, contact your firm choice university to discuss this with it. Universities may revise their offer and admit you if they still have places, or if you missed the grade by only a few marks it may ask you to try for a remark. Exam boards change the marks in only a few cases, though, and they can go down or up, so don't place all your hopes on this. If you still do not receive an offer from your firm choice university and have not received an offer from your insurance choice university, then call your insurance choice university. If, by the end of this process, you still have no offers, you will need to enter UCAS Clearing.

UCAS Clearing

Clearing is the name given to the system in which all remaining course vacancies are advertised on the UCAS website and in national newspapers. In Clearing, you contact the universities directly that have publicised course vacancies and give them your grades and UCAS ID number. If you think that you might need to use the Clearing system it is best to be well prepared because the vacancies are filled very quickly. Clearing is typically open from July to October.

Alongside their search tool, which includes over 30,000 course options, UCAS also offers Clearing matches, a tool that 'matches' candidates to a list of courses in UCAS Hub. If you find yourself in Clearing, it is advisable to check the 'See matches' button; if you find a course you like, select the 'I'm interested' button. If the university or college still has available places, they will contact you to discuss further and possibly make you an offer.

Advice for Clearing

- Make sure that you have your UCAS ID number and a copy of your UCAS application ready for results day.
- Remain proactive! Use the Clearing matches tool to speed up the process of finding another place.
- You need to have access to a phone that you can use exclusively, as you may need to make a lot of calls over the course of results day.
- You also need to have access to the internet in order to access the directory of courses available through Clearing on the UCAS website open. This is particularly useful as the website also has the university contact numbers that you will need to call.
- Think about the option of studying on courses that might not be identical to the one that you originally applied for, but are related. For example, sociology and psychology rather than single honours psychology.
- Be ready for an impromptu telephone interview. The admissions staff may ask why you want to study on the course, and you will need to have a little bit more tact than just saying 'because I didn't get into the course I really wanted to'. Instead you could say something like: 'Even though I didn't get in to my firm or insurance choices I did apply/intend to apply/visit during the open day/know that the course has a good student satisfaction rating in the *Guardian*, etc.'

If you decide to retake your A levels

If you have not achieved the grades that you needed for your chosen universities, and you do not want to take the available Clearing places, you could consider retaking one or more A levels. In the days when most examination boards offered January sittings, retaking might have meant studying for one term to boost the grade. The period from January to September could then be used to earn money, gain more work experience or travel the world. But, apart from international A levels, A level exams are now only available in June, and so retaking will involve studying for another year, so you need to be sure that your university aspirations are genuine enough to give you the motivation to add this extra year to your studies. As the A level system is now fully reformed, barring the last Phase Three legacy-subject examinations, you will need to retake the entire two-year qualification again and therefore plan to be able to do this in just a single year – you do not want a repeat of the examination if you are underprepared.

Speak to your teachers about the implications of retaking your exams. Some independent sixth-form colleges provide specialist advice and teaching for students. Interviews to discuss this are free and carry no obligation to enrol on a course, so it is worth taking the time to talk to their staff before you embark on A level retakes. Many further education colleges also offer retake courses, and some schools will allow students to return to resit subjects, either as external examination candidates or by repeating a year.

If you decide to reapply

Universities are usually happy to consider students who are reapplying, either because they did not get the required grades first time around, or because they did not receive any offers of places. It is worth contacting the university to check whether this is the case. Some will have policies on grade requirements for retake candidates, while others might ask for evidence of any extenuating circumstances that may have affected the previous application.

> **TIP!**
>
> - If there were extenuating circumstances that affected your application, include a brief mention of this in the personal statement ('I was disappointed not to have achieved the required grades, because my studies were affected by illness, but this has made me even more determined to become an engineer') but leave the details to the referee.
> - If you are retaking, you can use the extra term or extra year to add weight to your application, for example by gaining more work experience, taking up a new subject, enrolling in evening classes that are relevant to your application and furthering your reading.

10 | Fees and funding

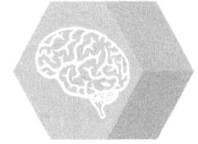

Even before you have secured a place at university, you will need to think about fees and funding. In this chapter we look at the different fee systems across the UK as well as the funding available. A comprehensive summary can be found in the 'Student finance' section on the UCAS website at: www.ucas.com/finance/undergraduate-tuition-fees-and-student-loans.

Fees

UK students

As the government of each of the UK home nations sets the fees that universities can charge, the tuition fee that you will have to pay for undergraduate courses will depend on where you live and where you intend to study. In England, only universities with a Teaching Excellence Framework (TEF) award and an access and participation plan (APP) from the Office for Students (OfS) are permitted to charge the maximum tuition fee. However, the TEF's impact on tuition fees is specific to England: it does not affect fee caps in Scotland, Wales or Northern Ireland.

The maximum tuition fee for the 2025/26 academic year was increased to £9,535. Prior to that, the fee cap had been frozen at £9,250 since the 2017/18 academic year. In the autumn of 2025, the UK government announced that, from 2026/27, university tuition fees in England are set to increase every year in line with inflation. The new tuition fee cap for students from England will be set at £9,790 for 2026 entry and £10,050 for 2027 entry.

There are a number of variations between the systems in England, Wales, Scotland and Northern Ireland, which can result in significant differences between the fees that are ultimately paid by students. The Welsh authorities have confirmed that they will implement the same tuition fee increase as England for the 2026/27 academic year, with the tuition fee cap for 2027/28 to be confirmed at a later date. At the time of writing (January 2026), Scotland and Northern Ireland are yet to confirm any plans to increase tuition fees for 2026/27 and beyond, so it is worth keeping an eye out in the news and on your regional student finance website for developments. For reference, this is the current situation regarding tuition fees:

- Students from England will be required to pay maximum fees of £9,790 for 2026/27, rising to £10,050 for 2027/28.
- Students from Wales will be required to pay maximum fees of £9,790 for 2026/27, with increases in subsequent academic years yet to be confirmed.
- Students from Scotland who study at Scottish universities are not required to pay tuition fees. However, Scottish students who choose to study in other UK nations are required to pay the tuition fees set by that country.
- Students living in Northern Ireland paid up to £4,855 to study in Northern Ireland in 2025/26. Northern Irish students who choose to study in other UK nations are required to pay the tuition fees set by that country.

EU and non-EU international students

EU students are charged the same fees as non-EU international students, which are significantly higher than those charged to UK students and are determined by each university. For example, at the University of Oxford, an EU or international student reading psychology would pay annual tuition fees of £54,990 for 2026 entry.

Some students from the EU may be eligible for some support in terms of student loans from the UK government, but this is dependent on a number of factors, so it is best to check personal eligibility. Students from the Republic of Ireland are exempt from paying higher fees and are eligible for home fee status.

Living expenses

Your living expenses include the cost of your accommodation, food, clothes, travel and equipment, leisure and social activities – plus possible extras like field trips and study visits, if these aren't covered by the tuition fees.

Check university and college websites for information about possible living costs. Some offer more detailed advice than others, and give breakdowns under various headings, such as accommodation, food and daily travel. Others go even further and give typical weekly, monthly or annual spends.

If you're living away from home, accommodation will make up the largest proportion of your living costs. There is likely to be a range of accommodation options – from a standard room in university halls through to privately rented accommodation – with a range of price points. You'll probably be surprised when you do some research to find that the cheapest and most expensive towns are not as you might have expected; the cost of accommodation often depends on how much of it is available in a particular area.

When choosing accommodation, it is essential to consider its location and factor in the cost of travel to your university or college. It is also important to find out what's included in the accommodation costs (such as utilities, personal property insurance and Wi-Fi) and whether it is possible to pay for accommodation during term time only.

Funding your studies

How do you fund your time in higher education? Don't ignore this question and leave it until the last minute! You will need to think carefully about how to budget for several years' costs – and you need to know what help you might get from:

- the government;
- your family or partner;
- paid part-time work;
- other sources, such as bursaries and scholarships.

This chapter gives a brief overview of a complicated funding situation, which can vary according to where you come from and where you plan to study. For more details about the different types of funding available and how to apply for them, check your regional student finance website.

- **England**: www.gov.uk/student-finance-england
- **Wales**: www.studentfinancewales.co.uk
- **Scotland**: www.saas.gov.uk
- **Northern Ireland**: www.studentfinanceni.co.uk

Tuition fee loans

For UK students, tuition fees can be covered by taking out a tuition fee loan, which will be paid directly to your university or college at the start of each year of your course. You are effectively given a loan by the government that you repay through your income tax after you finish your course but only once your earnings reach a certain threshold. For 2026/27, these income thresholds stand at:

- £25,000 per year for students from England (Plan 5);
- £29,385 per year for students from Wales (Plan 2);
- £33,795 per year for students from Scotland (who go to university outside of Scotland) (Plan 4);
- £26,900 per year for students from Northern Ireland (Plan 1).

(All figures apply to students starting their course after 1 August 2023).

You only have to start student loan repayments once your earnings exceed the relevant threshold. In addition, any outstanding balance on your loan will be cancelled after a certain period of time if you have not already cleared it in full. The length of time depends on the rules at the time you took out the loan. For students from England who started their studies in September 2023, the repayment period was recently extended to 40 years (from 30 years), so it is recommended that students in other regions keep a close eye on any developments with respect to the length of the loan repayment period. At the time of writing, the loan repayment term is 30 years for students from Wales and Scotland, and 25 years for students from Northern Ireland.

Loan repayments are set at 9% of anything you earn over the annual income threshold.

The interest rate charged on student loans depends on what repayment plan you are on, but for students in England on Plan 5 it is 3.2%.

Maintenance loans

In addition to a tuition fee loan, all students can apply for a maintenance or living cost loan, which is repayable in the same way. The amount you can borrow will be dependent on your household income – in other words, it is means tested. 'Household income' refers to your family's gross annual income (their income before tax). With the exception of loans available to Scottish students, the amount you can claim also varies depending on your living situation, with the maximum loan being available to students living away from home in London.

Each regional student finance website includes a finance calculator tool that will give an estimate of the finance you would be eligible for based on your family income and other factors, and it is well worth looking at this before planning your budget.

The UK government has announced that, from the 2026/27 academic year, maintenance loans for students from England will increase in line with inflation. Maintenance loans for Welsh students are also increasing; however, details of any additional support for students from Scotland and Northern Ireland for the 2026/27 academic year are yet to be confirmed. For reference, a summary of current maintenance support arrangements is given below.

England (2026/27)

The maximum annual maintenance loan in England:

- £9,118 for those living in the family home;
- £10,830 for those living away from home (£14,135 in London).

Wales (2026/27)

In Wales, students can get a combination of a maintenance grant, which they do not have to pay back, and a maintenance loan. Although the grants are means tested, most students should get a grant of at least £1,020.

The maximum amounts for maintenance loans and grants in Wales:

- £10,685 for those living in the family home;
- £12,590 for those living away from home (£15,720 in London).

Scotland (2025/26)

In Scotland, students can get a mix of maintenance loans and non-repayable bursaries (grants) to cover living expenses. These are as follows (all figures per year):

- Household income up to £20,999: £2,000 bursary and £7,000 loan;
- Household income £21,000–£23,999: £1,125 bursary and £7,000 loan;
- Household income £24,000–£33,999: £500 bursary and £7,000 loan;
- Household income £34,000 and above: no bursary and £6,000 loan.

Unlike the rest of the UK, bursaries and loan eligibility for Scottish students is calculated using the income bands listed above rather than exact household income.

In addition, a Special Support Loan of £2,400 is available to all full-time students. Unlike the maintenance loan and bursary, this is not means tested but it is repayable.

Northern Ireland (2025/26)

The maximum annual maintenance loan in Northern Ireland:

- £6,300 for those living in the family home;
- £8,132 for those living away from home (£11,391 in London).

In addition, you may be eligible for a non-repayable maintenance grant if your household income is below £41,065. This is paid alongside any maintenance loan you qualify for and is up to £3,475.

Alternative help with fees and funding

Financial hardship during your study

If you are struggling to cover costs once you have started a course, you may be eligible for hardship funding. The following funding pools are available.

- There are different hardship funds available for students in England, depending on the institution. English students should contact their college or university to check whether they will be eligible for extra funding.
- Maintenance Grant, the Welsh Government Learning Grant and Education Maintenance Allowance (Wales).
- Bursary/Educational Maintenance Grant (Scotland).
- Maintenance Grant and Special Support Grant (Northern Ireland).

Who gets what and how much is decided by individual course providers. You can usually access this by enquiring at your university's Student Services or student union.

Sponsorship

Commercial organisations, charitable trusts, educational institutions and government agencies all offer sponsorship, special grants, access funds and scholarships, but these sources of finance are limited and hard to come by. If you are facing financial difficulties, a good place to start looking for information is the institution that you are applying to. The UCAS website contains a section on funding, with contact details and links to a number of funding bodies: www.ucas.com/finance/additional-funding.

Funding for postgraduate courses

Students at this level are often self-funded or may be assisted by scholarships from universities or from other organisations. Contacting the institution to which you are applying is a good way to begin exploring your options.

In England, postgraduate loans are available up to £13,206 (2026/27) to help with the cost of the course fees and living costs. This funding does not depend on your personal income or your household income. The funding is available for both full-time and part-time postgraduate courses.

Studying overseas

More and more UK students are choosing to study overseas, and they can be divided into two main groups:

1. those whose courses at UK universities involve study abroad;
2. those who choose to apply to overseas universities, for example, in Europe, the United States, Canada or even further afield.

If you fall into the first category, you will be funded in the same way as outlined earlier in this chapter. If you fall into the second category, the fees will depend on where you are studying and on what course. It is unlikely that you will get a student loan or assistance with funding from within the UK for these courses, but many overseas universities offer scholarships for international students. A good starting point is to look at the Complete University Guide website: www.thecompleteuniversity guide.co.uk/student-advice/where-to-study/studying-abroad.

11 | Further information

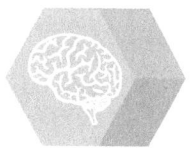

British Psychological Society (BPS)

The British Psychological Society (BPS) is the professional association for psychologists and is incorporated by Royal Charter. A Register of Chartered Psychologists was established in 1987, bringing a more organised and stricter discipline to the profession. Since 2009, professional psychologist titles are regulated by law and have to be registered with the Health and Care Professions Council. Chartered Psychologists are bound by an ethical code of conduct, which was set up to maintain the standards of psychology as a profession and to protect the public. The register lists members of the Society who have reached a certain standard in education and work experience. It contains their names, qualifications and work addresses. Chartered members can be found on the BPS website (www.bps.org.uk/lists/cpsychol).

The register is split into specialisms such as clinical, counselling, educational, forensic, health, occupational, sport and exercise, registered and practitioner psychologist. This is also reflected in the different divisions and sections of the memberships for each type of psychologist.

If you are a UK resident, to qualify for registration as a Chartered Psychologist you must:

- have achieved at least a 2.ii in an undergraduate honours degree accredited by the BPS that qualifies for Graduate Basis for Chartered Membership or completed a BPS-accredited conversion qualification, and
- have completed psychology research to doctoral level, or completed a BPS-accredited postgraduate qualification and training, or have postgraduate training and experience of teaching psychology, or have completed an assessment of competence in Coaching Psychology or the professional recognition route in Coaching Psychology.

Student membership of the BPS is open to everyone studying on a BPS-accredited undergraduate degree or conversion course. Members get the monthly magazines *The Psychologist* written by professionals and *PsychTalk* written by students, which, as well as articles and reports on a huge range of research, also carry job advertisements.

Students can also access a growing online community, which allows you to connect with other students across the UK, as well as enrol with your local branch where you can meet other psychologists and expand your professional network. Students have access to regular BPS events and career fairs, which provide opportunities to get advice from psychology professionals.

The BPS holds a directory of voluntary careers speakers who are members willing to go to schools and colleges to talk about careers in psychology. The BPS website also contains a wealth of information about becoming a psychologist.

For further information contact:

The British Psychological Society
St Andrews House
48 Princess Road East
Leicester LE1 7DR
www.bps.org.uk

Advance HE

Advance HE publishes an excellent guide to employability for psychology graduates. In their own words: 'This guide provides a psychology specific overview covering such topics as where psychology graduates work within and outside psychology, emerging areas of work, the job market, and includes activities to help you explore interests, skills, preferences and values.'

https://advance-he.ac.uk/knowledge-hub/psychology-student-employability-guide-0

Other useful organisations

Association for Coaching
Golden Cross House
8 Duncannon Street
London WC2N 4JF
www.associationforcoaching.com

Association of Educational Psychologists
4 The Riverside Centre
Frankland Lane
Durham DH1 5TA
www.aep.org.uk

British Association for Counselling and Psychotherapy
15 St John's Business Park
Lutterworth
Leicestershire LE17 4HB
www.bacp.co.uk

British Association of Sport and Exercise Sciences (BASES)
Rooms G07 and G08 Fairfax Hall
Leeds Beckett University
Headingley Campus
Leeds LS6 3QS
www.cases.org.uk

British Psychological Society Northern Ireland
Contact address as for main BPS
www.bps.org.uk/member-networks/northern-ireland-branch

British Psychological Society Scotland
Contact address as for main BPS
www.bps.org.uk/member-networks/scottish-branch

British Society of Criminology
The Nexus Building
Broadway
Letchworth Garden City
Hertfordshire SG6 9BL
www.britsoccrim.org

Chartered Institute of Personnel and Development (CIPD)
151 The Broadway
London SW19 1JQ
www.cipd.org

Health and Care Professions Council (HCPC)
184–186 Kennington Park Road
London SE11 4BU
www.hcpc-uk.org

Psychological Society of Ireland
Digital Office Centre Camden
12 Camden Row
Saint Kevin's
Dublin 8
D08 R9CN
Ireland
www.psychologicalsociety.ie

UK Council for Psychotherapy
York House
221 Pentonville Road
London N1 9UZ
www.psychotherapy.org.uk

General university guides

HEAP 2027: University Degree Course Offers, Brian Heap, 57th edition, Trotman

How to Complete Your UCAS Application, 2027 Entry, Ryan Moran & UCAS, 38th edition, MPW Guides/Trotman

The Essential Guide to UCAS Personal Statements, Dominic Fuge, 1st edition, Trotman

The University Choice Journal, Barbara Bassot, Trotman Education

University Interviews: Top answers and insider tips, Ian Stannard and Godfrey Cooper, Trotman Education

Psychology texts

As far as specific psychology textbooks go, any of the introductory texts found in large bookshops are fine. Those relating to social psychology are probably the easiest and most interesting to read if you are new to the subject.

Affective Neuroscience: The Foundations of Human and Animal Emotions, Jaak Panksepp, Oxford University Press

Atkinson and Hilgard's Introduction to Psychology, Susan Nolen-Hoeksema, Wadsworth

Classic Case Studies in Psychology, Geoff Rolls, Routledge

A Dictionary of Psychology (3rd edn), Andrew M. Colman, OUP

Emotional Intelligence, Daniel Goleman, Bloomsbury

The Essential Difference, Simon Baron-Cohen, Penguin

From the Edge of the Couch, Raj Persaud, Bantam

Genes and Behavior: Nature-Nurture Interplay Explained, Michael Rutter, Wiley-Blackwell

The Happiness Hypothesis, Jonathan Haidt, Basic Books

How the Mind Works, Stephen Pinker, Penguin

The Human Mind, Robert Winston, Bantam

Influence, New and Expanded: The Psychology of Persuasion, Robert B. Cialdini, Harper Business

The Jigsaw Man, Paul Britton, Corgi

The Little Book of Psychology, Emily Ralls & Caroline Riggs, Viva Editions

The Lucifer Effect: How Good People Turn Evil, Philip Zimbardo, Rider

Madness Explained: Psychosis and Human Nature, Richard P. Bentall, Penguin

The Man Who Mistook His Wife for a Hat, Oliver Sacks, Picador

Mapping the Mind, Rita Carter, Weidenfeld & Nicolson

Memory, How We Can Use It, Lose It and Can Improve It, David Samuel, Phoenix

The Moral Animal: The New Science of Evolutionary Psychology, Robert Wright, Abacus

The Noonday Demon: An Anatomy of Depression, Andrew Solomon, Chatto & Windus

Opening Skinner's Box: Great Psychological Experiments of the Twentieth Century, Lauren Slater, Bloomsbury

Penguin Dictionary of Psychology (4th edn), Allen, Reber and Reber, Penguin

Phobias: Fighting the Fear, Helen Saul, HarperCollins

QI: The Quest for Intelligence, Kevin Warwick, Piatkus

Thinking, Fast and Slow, Daniel Kahneman, Penguin

Tomorrow's People, Susan Greenfield, Penguin

Totem and Taboo (2nd edn), Sigmund Freud, Routledge

A User's Guide to the Brain, John Ratey, Abacus

Psychologies (magazine available from newsagents)

Useful websites

Advance HE: www.advance-he.ac.uk

British Association for Counselling and Psychotherapy: www.bacp.co.uk

ClinPsy: www.clinpsy.com

Health and Care Professions Council (HCPC): www.hcpc-uk.org

Graduate Careers Services Unit: https://luminate.prospects.ac.uk/

MIND: www.mind.org.uk

NHS: www.nhs.uk

NHS (mental health homepage): www.nhs.uk/conditions/stress-anxiety-depression

Neuroscience@nature.com: www.nature.com/subjects/neuroscience

Prospects: www.prospects.ac.uk

Psychology Today: www.psychologytoday.com

The Psychologist (BPS's monthly publication): https://www.bps.org.uk/psychologist

12 | Glossary

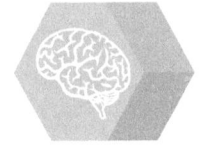

Behaviourism is an approach to psychology that sees all behaviour as a learned response to the environment.

Bipolar depression is a clinical disorder characterised by episodes of low mood as well as episodes of mania, among other characteristics.

Clinical and abnormal psychology concerns the definition, symptoms, classification and theories of different forms of mental illness.

Cognitive psychology covers the understanding of mental processes. It includes the study of memory, thinking and problem solving.

Cyberpsychology is an emerging field that studies human interactions with computers, phones and other electronic devices.

Depression is a clinical disorder characterised by episodes of low mood, among other characteristics.

Developmental psychology is the study of the process of human intellectual and emotional growth and development from birth to adulthood.

Evolutionary psychology focuses on the adaptive function of innate psychological characteristics and the role they may have played in human evolution.

Falsifiability is the principle that in hypothesis testing a proposition or theory cannot be considered scientific if it does not admit the possibility of being shown to be false.

Hallucination is a sensory experience that appears to be real but it is not, as it is created in the mind.

Maintenance loan is the money that the government will lend you to pay for your living expenses, such as rent, food and so on, depending on the UK region of your university and which region of the UK you are from. You will need to repay the loan when you complete your studies and are earning over the threshold amount of your repayment plan.

Mania is a heightened state characterised by great excitement, delusions and over-reactivity.

Neuropsychology looks at the relationship between the brain and nervous system and mental processes.

Parapsychology is the scientific study of psychic phenomena such as telepathy, spiritualism and extra-sensory perception.

Psychoanalysis is the type of psychotherapy that grew out of the theories and practice of Sigmund Freud.

Psychodynamics is the approach developed by Sigmund Freud and others seeking to understand personality, behaviour and abnormality through the interaction of conscious and unconscious processes.

Psycholinguistics involves the interface between psychology and language, its acquisition and structure.

Psychometrics is the measurement of attributes such as aptitude or personality, using psychological tests.

Psychopathology studies the origins, causes and development of psychological abnormalities and disorders.

Psychosocial relates to explanations based on a combination of social and behavioural factors.

Psychotherapy refers to the treatment of psychological abnormalities and disorders through psychological techniques.

Tuition fees loan is the money that the government will lend you to pay for your tuition fees. This money will not cover your living expenses, such as rent, food and so on. You will need to repay the loan when you complete your studies and are earning over the threshold amount of your repayment plan.

UCAS Clearing is the system through which all remaining course vacancies are advertised on the UCAS website and in national newspapers from July. Clearing is an important alternative for students who do not make the grade on results day. For more information see Chapter 9.

UCAS Extra is a service provided by UCAS for students who are not holding any offers/do not want to accept any offers.

UCAS Hub is the online portal through which you will receive your conditional offers, select which courses you would like to enrol on and find out whether you have got in on results day.

Abbreviations

ADD	Attention Deficit Disorder
ADHD	Attention Deficit Hyperactivity Disorder
ALF	Adult Learning Fund
APA	American Psychological Association
BA	Bachelor of Arts
BPS	British Psychological Society
BSc	Bachelor of Science
CAMHS	Child and Adolescent Mental Health Services
CBT	Cognitive Behavioural Therapy
CUG	The Complete University Guide
EEA	European Economic Area
EEG	Electroencephalography
EMDR	Eye Movement Desensitisation and Reprocessing
EP	Experimental psychology
EU	European Union
GBC	Graduate Basis for Chartered Membership
HCPC	Health and Care Professions Council
HECSU	Higher Education Careers Services Unit
MA	Master of Arts
MA SocSci	Master of Social Sciences
MBPsS	Graduate Member of the British Psychological Society
MPhil	Master of Philosophy
MRI	Magnetic resonance imaging
MSc	Master of Science
NHS	National Health Service
NSP	National Scholarship Programme
NUS	National Union of Students

OCD	Obsessive Compulsive Disorder
PEB	Psychology Education Board
PET	Positron emission tomography
PhD	Doctor of Philosophy
PPL	Psychology, Philosophy and Linguistics
PPS	Politics, Psychology and Sociology
PSI	Psychological Society of Ireland
QAA	Quality Assurance Agency
QTS	Qualified Teacher Status
RAE	Research Assessment Exercise
RCP	Royal College of Psychiatry
TQA	Teaching Quality Assessment
UCAS	Universities and Colleges Admissions Service

Have you seen the Getting into University series?

Get 30% off with code GET30

Our best-selling guides go beyond the official publications to give you expert, practical advice on how to successfully secure a place on the university course of your choice.

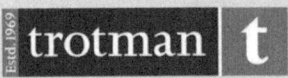

Order today from
www.trotman.co.uk/GettingInto